TRUE SELF

TRUE SELF

Connecting Passion, Purpose and Power

Jonathan Wells

For information please contact:
AdvancedLifeSkills.com

Book design by Jonathan Wells

ISBN   1453843337
EAN-13 9781453843338

"You already possess all the passion,
purpose and power you will ever need.
Learning to fully connect with these amazing
inner qualities will transform your life forever."

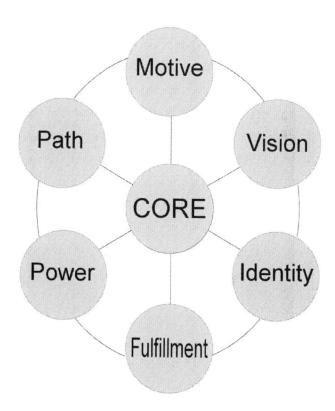

Contents

Designing Success - *Path Connection*

Harness the Power - *Power Connection*

Accept Success - *Identity Connection*

Life is Circular - *Fulfillment Connection*

Introduction

Are you happy right now, or are you busy pursuing happiness? Is your life fulfilling and satisfying today, or is that a reward that you have attached to some future goal or accomplishment? Do you feel that better circumstances will somehow open the door to living a more meaningful life?

If your answers to these questions put happiness, satisfaction and fulfillment just out of reach, you should not be too surprised. Our society and the people in it are suffering from a chronic condition I call Core Disconnection Disorder (CDD).

As a people we seem to have lost our connection with our deepest core values and passions. Simple, basic human needs like the ability to feel happy, satisfied, and fulfilled have become elusive concepts that are pursued but rarely attained.

Is any of this resonating with you? If so, the solution might be closer than you realize. In fact, I believe that you already have most of the components necessary for a happy and fulfilling life. It might feel like these things are missing from your life, but they are not really missing. In truth, they are simply waiting to be discovered.

This book is about making those very essential connections. It's a step by step approach to unlocking your amazing potential by mobilizing some of your most powerful core assets. TRUE SELF is a progressive path designed to align your deepest passions with your core values and innermost sense of purpose.

This book is about connecting with the real you, your TRUE SELF.

Dedicated to my amazing wife Pattie who has always believed in me and whose love and loyalty inspire me to become a better person.

Section 1 - Core Connection

Real Self

About Section 1

The core connection is about finding out who you really are on the deepest levels. It is structured to help you discover your real self. Included are specific exercises designed to help your connect with your most powerful core assets.

Please be sure to do the exercises as you come to them. The power to quickly transform your life begins with the information revealed in these exercises.

Make sure you write your answers down either in the space provided or in a separate notebook so you can refer back to them throughout the program.

If you skip the exercises, the information in this program will not have the same powerful impact on your life that you deserve. So please - take the time to invest in your own transformation by completing each exercise as you come to it.

Chapters 1-6

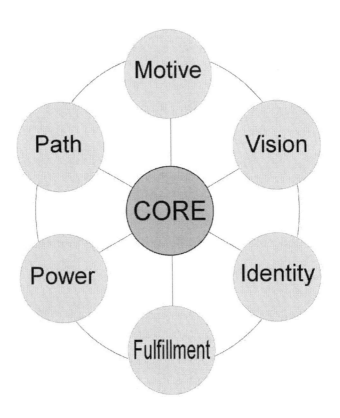

Chapter 1 -

Internal Harmony

Everything that we do, say and think is in some way an expression of our internal state. When we are at peace with ourselves we tend to be at peace with those around us. Internal harmony is a resourceful and comfortable reference point that allows us to relax and be at ease in our surroundings.

On the other hand, when there is conflict and discord from within, our world seems agitated and unsettled.

Our perception of life will always reflect the degree of internal harmony we are experiencing.

Have you ever noticed how much less irritating people and situations seem when you are in a really good mood? Is that because the world around you decided to behave itself and cut you some slack, or was it something else?

Have you ever blamed stress for a less than resourceful response to a minor challenge? We've all experienced similar fluctuations.

In such situations our tendency is to pass it off as:

- A good day or a bad day.
- Feeling either relaxed or stressed out.
- Things went well or everything went wrong.

Did you notice what all of those reasons have in common? They all give credit for our response to an external force, don't they? Each one of those reasons says, "It's not me, it wasn't my fault, I couldn't help it."

We can learn a great deal about the condition of our internal equilibrium if we think of our response patterns as clues. As my friend John likes to say, "if nothing is random then everything is a clue." Think about the life altering implications of acknowledging that simple truth.

If you've ever raised a child you know that a cranky two-year-old often just needs a nap. How do you know that? It's because you've learned to recognize the symptoms. Their response pattern serves as a clue to a seemingly unrelated problem.

Did the child ever think that he needed a nap? Not a chance, but experience told you otherwise, didn't it?

When we're cranky, do we just need a nap? Well maybe, or we might think we need a vacation, a day off, or some down time.

In reality they all mean the same thing. The not-so-subtle message here is, "I need to restore my internal harmony." Each of us has a built-in sense of emotional equilibrium. When things get out of balance we can't help but feel it on some level. It's important to recognize that the more complicated and hectic life becomes, the harder it is to maintain this balance.

For example, you're probably familiar with the concept of information overload. Have you ever wondered how much information is too much? At what point does it have a negative effect on our sense of equilibrium? Where is the line between satisfying our natural desire to know, and feeling weighed down?

I can't answer that with a statistic but I can offer a comparison. There is more information in one Sunday edition of the New York Times newspaper, than the average person living 200 years ago would have taken in during their entire lifetime. That's a staggering contrast, don't you think?

This simple example illustrates the need for all of us to

develop strategies and skills that will help us maintain our sense of harmony and balance.

At a time when the world around us is saying, "do more, do it faster, hurry up, earn more, spend more, don't get left behind," it's up to you to establish balance and harmony in your own life.

If you want to avoid getting lost in the noise, then the place to start is by identifying who you really are on the deepest levels. In this first section we are going to clear away all the trappings and take a close look at the real you, your true self.

Internal harmony cannot coexist with internal conflict. If your passions are out of sync with your values, there will be conflict. If your beliefs about what you are capable of do not support your goals, there will be conflict.

Even though the world around us has changed with the passage of time, the basic core desire of every person on the planet has always been the same. What is it that we really want above all else? What basic need is the driving force behind almost every human endeavor?

The answer is simple; we all want to be happy. We seek love, security, wealth and approval because we hope that they will make us happy.

Happiness starts on the inside. People and things may bring a degree of joy to our lives, but true and lasting happiness is a product of inner peace. It seems so ironic that internal harmony, which is the very foundation for happiness, is perhaps the most neglected of all human pursuits.

Unless we take the time to identify our true self, examine our values, passions, beliefs and motives, we cannot possibly find real happiness. It has been said that the quality of your life is in direct proportion to the quality of your ability to communicate effectively. Meaningful communication begins with self.

How many problems in the world are the direct results of poor communication? Marriages fail; businesses collapse and wars are fought because there was a breakdown in communication. What degree of depression, anger, frustration and self-sabotaging behavior is actually due to a breakdown of internal communication?

In the chapters that follow we are going to unravel the mystery of who you are. Not only will we identify your true self, but you will also learn how to adjust the many different aspects of the internal 'You' until they harmonize with one another. Then and only then will we move on to other endeavors.

Everything in this program is built on the foundation of establishing and maintaining internal harmony. Even when we move into the realm of personal success and goal setting, we will always consider how they affect our inner harmony.

Here's the bottom line for this first chapter: it is not possible to find true happiness and satisfaction in your pursuits without first establishing internal harmony. If you circumvent this vital step your results will suffer.

Somewhere inside yourself, behind the noise and confusion is the real you, your true self. Working together we will identify and define who you really are. In this first section we will lay the groundwork for an extraordinary journey of exceptional personal growth and unprecedented change. Are you ready?

Chapter 2 -

Personal Values

Personal values play a huge role in a person's ability to reach their goals and achieve success in life. If you do not take the time to figure out what your standards and values are, you can easily undermine your own success without even realizing it.

I am not just talking about success in business. I'm talking about living a successful life. This includes your personal sense of self-worth, level of self-confidence, and the depth of joy and satisfaction you experience.

If you want to have a truly worthwhile and abundant life, you must be clear on what is right and what is wrong according to your personal code of ethics.

When we want something in life, there is a tendency to justify our actions and excuse behavior that is out of harmony with our deepest sense of right and wrong. We may not even know we are doing it on a conscious level, or we may minimize the situation telling ourselves, "It's no big deal."

The problem is, on a deeper level we have created an internal battleground of conflict. If we allow ourselves to continue without correcting the problem, sooner or later that internal conflict will undermine our efforts and we will be forced to compensate.

How will we compensate? It could be in any number of ways. We may end up self-sabotaging our own success. We may turn to excesses in an effort to drown out our emotional discomfort. Even if we manage to succeed on some level, the success we experience will be a hollow one, lacking a sense of true joy and accomplishment.

No matter how it plays out, an exceptional life filled with joy in abundance is only possible if we conduct ourselves within the boundaries of our personal code of ethics. To do that we need to get clear on what is acceptable and what is unacceptable. That means we need to figure it out, and then write it down.

That might sound easy, but there's a little more to it. You see, for us to get past our tendency to rationalize our own behavior, we need to discover why we feel something is right or wrong. Why it's okay to do one thing, but not okay to do something else.

The best way to approach this is not by creating a long list of rules. A much better approach is to develop a short list of the guiding principles that can be applied to every aspect of our lives. Let me illustrate the difference between rules and principles.

In the U.S. thousands of new rules, laws, ordinances, regulations and codes are added to the law books every year in an attempt to regulate how people treat one another. Now let's compare the hundreds of thousands of written laws with one guiding principle. This principle is often referred to as the Golden Rule, which basically says that we should treat others the way we would like them to treat us.

If everyone followed that simple principle we would not need all of those thousands of rules and laws. Obviously, it would be next to impossible to get billions of people to live by a few good principles. But we are not talking about billions of other people, we are only talking about one person, you.

So here is the challenge. If you put some thought into it, you should be able to come up with 3-5 guiding principles that will allow you to pursue your goals and passions, while staying true to your personal values and standards. Taking the time required to put those principles into writing and then allowing yourself to be guided by them will pave the way for a life of internal peace and harmony.

I realize that without examples it can be difficult to come up with principles to guide your life. So let's consider a few areas where your guiding principles will play an important role and then we'll look at a few examples.

Keep in mind that guiding principles are not rules, so you don't want to create a list of rules to follow. For our purposes, they are intentions much like the ones you will create in the goal setting section of this program. Your guiding principles will define the way you intend to conduct yourself in a wide variety of situations. They are something to strive for, not something to limit you.

For starters, you will want to have some guiding principles that help you determine how you will treat and react to other people in general. Having a loving, kind, nonjudgmental approach to other people could form the basic structure for a guiding principle in this area.

Keep in mind, that showing respect for others does not necessarily mean that you're okay with the things that they do. It simply means that, while you may not agree with some of their actions, you don't judge them as a person. It's very important to distinguish between the person and their actions.

How might we apply the Golden Rule to a guiding principle that outlines the way we will deal with other people? We can start by stating our intention to treat others the way we would like them to treat us.

All of us prefer to be treated with respect and consideration. So, why not make it your determination to treat others that way? We also like to be given the benefit of the doubt, so naturally you'll want to avoid jumping to conclusions. Additionally, none of us likes to be spoken to harshly or disrespectfully, so perhaps you will want to accord others the same kindness.

Let's incorporate those elements into a guiding principle and see what it would look like. Remember, this is just an example to help you get started.

Sample Guiding Principle for How I Treat Others:

> I will always treat others with the same level of respect and consideration that I would like to receive from them. I will endeavor to demonstrate this by showing them kindness and respect when I speak to them or about them, even if we don't agree on certain issues.

See how easy that was? Now let's work on a guiding principle to address the way you treat yourself. Obviously, you want to treat yourself with at least the same level of consideration that you show to others.

The goal here is to design a principle that will build up your inner sense of approval by showing self-respect. When we constantly run ourselves down or belittle ourselves, it undermines our self-esteem and self-confidence. So you want a guiding principle designed to build you up in these areas.

Many people find that simply eliminating negative self-talk also helps them feel a lot better about themselves. Let's combine these elements and see how we might design a guiding principle in this area.

Again, this is only meant to be an example.

Sample Guiding Principle for How I Treat Myself:

> I am a valuable person and will treat myself as such. When I make a mistake it's not a reflection on my intelligence or my worth as a human being. It is just a mistake. I will always treat myself with respect and compassion because I deserve it.

Other important areas of your life where you might want to have some guiding principles could include: work and recreation, diet and exercise, friend and family relationships, spirituality and anything else that's important to you personally.

Okay, now it's your turn. Take a sheet of paper and spend a few minutes jotting down some thoughts. Start by making a list of your values. What kind of standards do you want to live by? What are your personal ethics? These are terms we don't hear very often these days, values, standards and ethics, so perhaps you haven't given it much thought in the past.

The goal here is to come up with 3-5 guiding principles that you personally are willing to live by because they represent who you are as a person. Please don't underestimate the importance of this exercise; it is a very valuable lesson in personal discovery.

To achieve a life of personal excellence you absolutely need to be clear about who you are and what you stand for. So don't try to rush the process and don't shortchange yourself. Even if you need to think about it for several days it's worth whatever amount of time you can invest.

This is probably the hardest assignment in this entire book. It is the foundation upon which you will begin building a life of exceptional quality.

Once you have your list of guiding principles, write them in your book or on a separate sheet of paper so you can refer back to them as we continue.

Please don't skip the following exercise!

It's imperative to your success with everything that follows!

"Live one day at a time
emphasizing ethics rather than rules."
-Wayne Dyer

My Guiding Principles for Internal Harmony

1) I am a good human being. When I
make a mistake it's nothing to be
ashamed of. I will treat myself
with love and respect because I am
worthy and deserving of it.

2) I will tolerate others and show
kindness, even I disagree with them

3) I will think positively, even if I am
thinking too much and dont place
value in others opinions, only mines.

4) Just because society, strangers or even
neighbours reject me doesn't mean
I am unworthy, bad and alone person.
I am not alone. I have friends and
family who love and support me.

5)

Most people allow the world around them or their current circumstances to dictate what is acceptable and what is not. What you want to do is to establish and live by values that represent a higher standard for you as an individual.

Don't let your life become a contest to see how much you can get away with without getting caught. The fruitage of that kind of mindset is all too obvious in society today - don't be deceived by it. The only way to protect yourself from the demoralizing effect of those who choose the low road is to establish a higher road and then be determined to stay on it

By establishing your own personal code of ethics, you are deciding what caliber of person you will allow yourself to be. Your guiding principles for internal harmony will provide you with a yardstick by which you can measure your thoughts, words and actions. Being true to a higher standard will bring a deep sense of satisfaction and peace to your life.

Instead of being held back by internal conflict or sabotaged by internal disharmony, you will be empowered by your own commitment to your personal values. So, if you skipped the exercise, please go back and complete it now. Do it for you!

Chapter 3 -

Paradigms of Pain & Pleasure

Almost all of the choices we make in our daily life are motivated by one of two powerful forces. The most powerful of these forces is the desire to avoid pain. The second is the desire for pleasure.

Everything that we want to do is something we have emotionally linked to pleasure. Everything we try to avoid doing is something we have linked to pain. These are the two main paradigms of life, and we have an emotional association for everything in our life that we have attached to one of these two categories.

Sometimes our willpower and logic try to do battle with these two powerful forces, but any logic-based victory is usually short-lived. Here's an example: Almost every cigarette smoker I've ever met knows that smoking is bad for him. He knows that he would be better off if he stopped smoking. So why does he keep smoking? Because emotionally, smoking represents pleasure and quitting represents pain.

The only way for a smoker to stop smoking is to learn to associate pain to his habit and pleasure to quitting.

This requires having a long-term point of view, rather than a short-term, instant gratification viewpoint. The very thing that brings him pleasure in the short term will bring him pain in the long run. It all depends on your point of reference, your paradigm.

I used smoking as an example because the harmful effects are universally recognized, but we could apply the same analogy to a wide variety of choices that we make on a daily basis.

Exercise could be considered painful in the short term but the long-term benefits are very desirable. If eating represents one of your greatest pleasures, then the very thought of dieting would represent pain. So, for some people, exercising and dieting is a double dose of pain, and yet logically, they realize that this is the fastest path to physical fitness. It's a tug-of-war between emotions and logic.

Understanding how these two powerful forces work in our personal life is the first step toward taking control of our own destiny. We can actually learn how to use our minds to program our emotional associations. In other words, we decide our own paradigms. We can choose what is painful and what is pleasurable.

Many things in our lives influence what we view as painful, and what we view as pleasurable. Paradigms, however, are about association; they are about our own interpretation. Learning to program our emotional response is a vital step in our personal development.

There are a couple of things that I'd like to clarify regarding our emotional desire to seek pleasure and avoid pain. It's not the actual pain or pleasure that drives us, but our estimate of it. For example, our desire to avoid pain is really our fear of taking any action that we feel may lead to pain. Likewise, it's not the actual pleasure that motivates us to take action, but our belief that a certain action will lead to a pleasurable experience. It's all about perception.

Have you ever noticed that the anticipation of pain that we think might result from a certain action is generally much worse than the actual experience? Here's an example: If you've ever done any public speaking it's usually the 10-15 minutes before you get on stage that creates the greatest anxiety. You may experience an increased heart rate, a rise in body temperature and a nauseous feeling in your stomach. All this is caused by your estimation of what the experience will be like, not by the actual experience.

Speaking from my own personal experiences and those of other public speakers I know, everyone agrees that the anxiety that comes beforehand generally vanishes as soon as they begin speaking. Anxiety, of course, is simply a form of fear.

Fear always fits into one or more of these three main categories.

1. A desire for approval
2. A desire for control
3. A desire to feel secure

If you examine any fear, whether it's the fear of rejection, fear of failure, or fear of loss, you'll find that it fits into one or more of these three categories.

Take the example of our public speaker. Once he gets on stage and focuses on his topic, he can settle down and enjoy the experience. But during the 10 to 15 minutes before he gets on stage, he is not thinking about his topic. Instead, he is focused on himself. He is wondering if he'll have the approval of his audience, if he'll have control of his voice and body language, and the anxiety is making him feel insecure.

The solution is to focus on the outcome, the feeling of satisfaction and approval that will come from a job well done. By visualizing a pleasurable outcome there is a complete shift of focus. Excitement replaces anxiety and the expectation of pleasure replaces fear. Moving toward a desirable result is an enjoyable experience. It is something to anticipate and look forward to.

Now we see that one way to avoid pain and move toward pleasure is simply to change our focus. In our example, a short-term focus created pain in the form of fear and anxiety, while a long-term focus turned the whole experience into a pleasurable one.

> "When you become the master of your focus
> you can decide whether an experience
> will be painful or pleasurable."

We would all like to think that we make up our own minds as to what is pleasurable and what is painful. In reality, we are constantly being conditioned by our environment to link certain things with pain or pleasure. Advertisers study human behavior in an effort to link their products to our emotions. Their advertising campaigns are designed to create subconscious emotional associations or links, and they do so without our conscious awareness.

The attitudes of our close associates also have a powerful influence on our personal paradigms. Their opinions can actually precondition us to view things the way that they do. We may value someone else's opinion so much that we subconsciously adopt their viewpoint, without having any personal experience.

Trying to gain the approval of an individual, or a group, can also shape our preferences. In such cases we find that our acceptance will often hinge on our ability to conform to the group opinion.

Stereotypes can also have a powerful influence. Our minds tend to group similar experiences into general categories. If we encounter a new experience that seems to fit into one of these categories that has always resulted in pain, we will likely expect this new experience to be painful as well.

For example: If every time you try to go on vacation you wind up having car trouble, in the future you will probably expect more of the same. The very thought of taking a vacation may conjure up an image of being stuck on the side of the road, waiting for a tow truck. As a result, an activity designed to bring you pleasure now represents pain.

"I have learned that the greater part of our misery or unhappiness is determined not by our circumstance but by our disposition."
- Martha Washington

The important point to remember here is that we need to develop the ability to decide for ourselves what we will view as pleasurable and what we will view as painful. If we don't take control of this process, then the world around us will take over our internal programming. Instead of controlling our environment, we will come to be controlled by it. Because the pain/pleasure dynamic has such a powerful influence on our lives, we owe it to ourselves to take personal responsibility for how we choose to view things.

Whenever something happens in your life, your brain will ask two questions. First, is this going to bring me pain or pleasure? Second, what must I do now to avoid the pain and or gain the pleasure? How you interpret the situation will determine your answers. In addition, it will also form the foundation for your future expectations.

Where do our passions come from?
Is it true that we have no control over who
or what we fall in love with? Let's find out...

Chapter 4 -

Choosing Your Passions

Our culture and the demands of modern living have a way of homogenizing our dreams and aspirations as we grow up. When we are children, it's easy to fantasize about becoming the manifestation of our passions when we grow up.

As children our dreams are not limited by the negative "better face reality" attitudes that tend to stifle our imaginations as the years go by. Children don't see a wall between reality and fantasy and that is a truly beautiful way to think.

When a little girl says, "Mommy, I want to be a ballerina when I grow up," she means it. Children are, and should be, full of passion and enthusiasm about whom they want to become in the future. As parents, we try to encourage those kinds of feelings, don't we?

If you fast forward twenty years it seems that very few of those little girls grew up to realize their childhood dreams. Otherwise, the world would have a lot more ballerinas.

Why is that? What prevented them from fulfilling those childhood dreams?

Is it because now they are pursuing other passions? Sometimes that is the reason and it's perfectly normal for our passions to change as we grow and learn.

Unfortunately, more often than not, those dreams and fantasies have been replaced with a more middle-of-the-road reality.

Now, life certainly doesn't need to be glamorous to be fulfilling, that's not the point. Any life that fulfills your dreams and passions is a life worth living. The trouble is that many people's lives are devoid of passion. Their dreams seem like impossible fantasies and they have set them aside and learned to focus on just getting by.

Again, there is nothing wrong with a simple life or just getting by, if that feels fulfilling to you. A simple life can still be full of simple passion.

Actually, this brings up a very important point about the role of passion in your life. The more you can develop a passion for the everyday activities in your life, the greater your sense of joy, satisfaction and fulfillment will be.

Notice, I said, "develop a passion." Our emotional response to anything can be positive, negative or neutral. The more positive the response, the easier it is to develop a feeling of passion and enthusiasm in that direction.

Here's the point, we can control and adjust our emotional response to anything, if we choose to. By doing so, we can develop and cultivate our feelings of passion and enthusiasm.

Think of the implications here. Everyone's life involves spending sizable blocks of time taking care of average, everyday activities.

If you are a woman with a family, how many meals do you make in a month? How much time do you devote to cleaning and shopping? How do you feel about those activities?

Now, imagine what your life would feel like if you looked forward to doing those things, if you had a passion for them. You're probably thinking "yeah right, this guy must be nuts." For the sake of discussion, just humor me for a moment.

Instead of responding from your current feelings about such things, let yourself pretend that these activities fill you with joy. Imagine that you actually look forward to each day with enthusiasm and passion even if you know that it is going to be full of mundane activities and chores.

Go ahead and close your eyes for a minute and let that scenario play out in your mind. See yourself enjoying every aspect of your day's activities, with a song in your heart and a smile on your face. Now, allow yourself to linger there for a minute.

As unlikely as it might seem that you could actually feel that way, wasn't it a nice thought? Didn't it feel great to really enjoy the things you needed to do anyway?

Okay, here's the deal. It doesn't matter if you are a housewife, a high-powered executive, a teacher or a personal trainer. Two things are true in your life and mine, no matter how you spend your time.

1) Life is full of repetitive activities that need to be done.
2) You can gain a great deal of personal satisfaction and joy by programming your emotions to truly enjoy these everyday activities.

Your internal emotional response to your life is a personal choice. By mastering a few simple skills you can choose to fill your life with passion and joy.

There is another great benefit to learning these skills.

Sometimes people find themselves inadvertently cultivating a desire for things that are out of harmony with their beliefs and values. Wrong desires are the foundation of untold pain and suffering. So much of what is wrong in the world today started out with someone acting on an inappropriate passion or desire.

Such actions never lead to a truly satisfying life of exceptional quality. Instead, they rob you of your dignity and destroy your sense of self-esteem.

But remember, you have a choice. The same skills that allow you to assign a positive emotional value to average daily activities also give you the power to devalue unwanted or inappropriate tendencies.

Doing so will make it possible for you to choose to be passionate about things that support your personal values and to discard anything that offends those values.

When you choose to be the one who decides what you will be passionate about, you become the master of your own world and the designer of your own life.

The quality of our life is more about what we make of it than what our current circumstances are. Really, it's all about attitude.

Circumstances have a way of changing. Sometimes they support our dreams and passions while at other times they provide a challenge. The ability to keep your dreams alive in the face of challenging circumstances is one of the greatest attributes of a successful person.

When your passions are in harmony with your values and beliefs, obstacles become opportunities and walls become hurdles that you can jump over.

Mastering your passions is the first step toward mastering your life.

Have you found your passions in life or are you still searching? Believe it or not, many times people are already living a life of passion without recognizing it. Could that be true for you?

Passion is the fuel that can power you toward the realization of your dreams. To live a truly satisfying and purposeful life, you need to know what your passions are so you can fill your day with them.

With that in mind, here's a little exercise. Take a sheet of paper and make a list of everything and anything that you feel passionate about. Don't analyze your feelings; just write them down as rapidly as you can.

If it's something that makes you feel happy, write it down. Anything that you can get excited about, write it down. Big things, little things, they all matter, physical things and emotional things alike.

It could be something exceptional like a vacation to Fiji or something simple like a smile from a loved one. Think about your favorite foods, movies, or restaurants. Maybe it's something you did years ago or something you want to do in the future. If it makes you feel happy, if it makes you feel passionate, then write it down.

The following questions will guide you through the process of discovering your passions. Why not write each question on its own sheet of paper so you have plenty of room for brainstorming. Many people wonder, "How do I know what my passions are?"

→ **Use the seven questions below to put your passion to the test.**

1) Does it make you feel good about yourself?
2) Would you do it for free?
3) Do you lose all track of time when you do it?
4) Do you talk about it to anyone who will listen?
5) Are you delighted to teach it to others?
6) Would you like to spend more of your time doing it?
7) Does it make you want to get out of bed in the a.m.?

Answering these seven questions will allow you to correctly identify what really excites you in your life. If you find something that meets all seven of these criteria, then it is definitely something that you are really passionate about.

We all have passions. Sometimes we just need to clear our minds, ask some simple questions and then give ourselves a little creative space. Why not start identifying your own passions right now? Do the exercise, apply these seven questions and watch the discovery process unfold.

This exercise is designed to help you discover what your passions are, not to make judgments about them. Write as quickly as you can and try to keep writing until you have at least 30 things on your list. If you get blocked, go for a walk or look at some old picture albums. Go to the store and look at the cover of the magazines. Look at the travel magazines or photography magazines. Do whatever it takes, but don't read past this paragraph until you have your list of at least 30 things that get you excited, or that make you feel passionate.

"When work, commitment, and pleasure all become one and you reach that deep well where passion lives, nothing is impossible." -Unknown Author

Okay, now that you have your list, go back and read it out loud. As you do, notice how it makes you feel. Have you discovered or rediscovered your passions?

Now let's go back and work on your list for a minute. The goal here is to pick out the 10 items on your list that make you **feel** the best. Don't be concerned with the value of those 10 items according to any other criteria. This is about what makes you feel best.

A passion is a feeling, it's an emotional response, and that makes it personal. There are no right choices, and there are no wrong choices. Simply pick the ones that make you feel the best.

Try to do this quickly without overanalyzing each item on your list. Your first impression is probably a better indicator of your feelings than anything else. If any one item on your list makes you feel happier, more excited, especially enthusiastic, or just brings a smile to your face more than the others, choose that one.

Now write those top 10 feel-good items in your book or on a separate sheet of paper in any order you want, so that you will be able to refer back to them as we go along. Use a pencil rather than a pen in case you need to make any changes later.

My Top 10 Passions

1)_____
_____
_____
_____

2)_____
_____
_____
_____

3)_____
_____
_____
_____

4)_____
_____
_____
_____

5)_____
_____
_____
_____

6)_____
_____
_____
_____

7)_____

_____

_____

_____

8)_____

_____

_____

_____

9)_____

_____

_____

_____

10)_____

_____

_____

_____

This list and the feelings that it stimulates will prove to be an invaluable tool for bringing passion to otherwise mundane activities, so please, make sure you complete this exercise before moving on.

> Do you ever find yourself having an emotional response that defies your logical assessment of the situation? Would you like to know why?

Chapter 5 -

Response Patterns

Here's what established response patterns are, and why it is so important to understand how they influence us.

An established response pattern starts with a mental recording of a personal experience and your emotional response to it. Every single experience you have provides information to your nervous system through some or all of your five senses: sight, taste, hearing, touch and smell. This information is recorded as a memory.

When you experience similar events over and over again, you form familiar neurological pathways or grooves.

The more repetitive the experience, the deeper and more established the grooves become. It is the equivalent of a neural roadway, an established route for neurological communication. This is a physical process where one neuron communicates with another neuron in a neural pathway.

Today, when you experience some event, your brain instantly searches its recorded memories in an attempt to recognize an established pattern. Within milliseconds it can replay a memory from a similar experience.

When this happens, you basically go on autopilot, feeling the same way, and doing the same or similar things you have done perhaps hundreds or even thousands of times before.

This is why you often feel and act the same ways in similar situations. Established response patterns form the foundations of all our habits and personality traits. Not only do they play a vital role in our survival, but they also make our behavior somewhat predictable.

Unfortunately, as important as established response patterns are to our survival, they can also make us feel and act in ways that do not support our efforts at personal development. In addition, they make it very difficult to change unwanted or undesirable habits.

Here are 4 examples of how an established response pattern can undermine a person's ability to succeed in making long-term changes:

1) A salesperson struggles with low self-esteem. His feelings stem back to his youth when he was routinely told that he was stupid and would not amount to anything. Now as an adult, he may feel personally rejected and become despondent because of missing a sale. So on every call, instead of feeling excited over the possibility of a new business relationship; there is a feeling of fear, and the anticipation of failure. Sadly, this poor man can't figure out why.

2) A former smoker may feel an overpowering urge to light up when seeing an old smoking buddy, or when visiting a place that simply looks similar to an old hangout where he used to smoke a lot. He feels there is little he can do to stop the urge except leave, because the emotional trigger for smoking is linked to these people or places.

3) An overweight person may have been given praise or rewards, like dessert, for eating everything on her plate as a child. This created a link in her nervous system that food equals pleasure, acceptance and love, regardless of the fact that she now recognizes the unhealthy consequences. So, no matter how hard she tries to stick with a diet, she is compelled by her desire for approval to return to her old eating habits.

4) A person suffering from social anxiety could have been teased unmercifully as a child, possibly even being labeled with a "nickname" because of a weight problem, crooked teeth or even because of one embarrassing event. Now, years later, even though this person may be skinny, have straightened teeth, and gone through years of therapy, they could still experience a panic attack when they are in the company of strangers.

We all have thousands of subconscious, established response patterns like these. Some are empowering and some are limiting. Without our being aware of it, these patterns exert a constant influence on our thoughts, emotions and actions.

Established response patterns are outside of our normal thought process and therefore easily override logic. When someone responds to a situation in a way that doesn't seem to make any sense at all, established response patterns are often the reason.

These are the hidden forces that sway our emotions and influence our decisions. They operate subtly, like an emotional riptide below the surface. They are the leftover and forgotten responses to events and situations that no longer exist on a conscious level.

Efforts to bury them do not remove their power. Attempting to nullify them with reason and logic does not work either. So what can we do?

Here's the good news. If reading this information helped you to become aware of some of your own limiting response patterns, there is no reason to be overly concerned. In the next chapter we will explore several effective ways to dismantle them and break free of their influence.

Once again, this is an area where learning and applying a few simple skills can literally transform the quality of your life experience.

"When we develop the ability to use our logical minds to harness and direct the power of our emotions - that is the moment when we truly begin to take control of our life."

The next chapter is the longest and one of the most powerful in this entire program. We are going to cover practical ways to modify and channel the power of some of your greatest assets.

Important Notice about the Next Chapter

Your beliefs form the very core of who you are as a person. They determine your level of self-esteem and your quality of life in general. The way you see the world and the way you see yourself in that world has everything to do with what you believe.

Simply put, beliefs can be your greatest asset or worst liability.

The next chapter is designed to bring you face to face with your own belief systems and the emotional anchors behind them. Doing so will make it possible to fully identify your true self as promised by the title of this book.

There is a lot of information and some important exercises coming up. To enjoy the full transformational power of this program you really need to cover this information thoroughly.

Individually, each of the seven sections in this book can stand alone. But the real power is in the synergy and identifying your beliefs is fundamental for everything that follows.

Please be willing to spend whatever time and energy it takes to fully benefit from the next chapter. I promise that you will be forever grateful.

Chapter 6 -

Modifying Your Beliefs

Realize it or not, our personal beliefs play a huge role in how we view our own life. Your estimation of your successes and failures will depend entirely on the framework of your personal belief system. What do I mean by the phrase "belief system"?

A belief system is a structured process by which we evaluate everything in our lives. We develop our own personal belief system based on how we interpret the world around us according to our observations and experiences.

There are two major components or aspects that contribute to your personal beliefs, an emotional component and a logical component.

In some cases, a belief may start out much like a theory where assumptions are made based on logical observations and deductions. In other cases it may grow out of an emotional viewpoint that seems to be supported by logic.

The blending of these two major components forms the foundation of our personal belief system. We employ these beliefs as we try to make sense out of the things going on around us. We also use them to form assumptions about probable future results. Once established, beliefs exert a powerful influence on our ability to achieve success in life.

Belief systems can run the full range from empowering to disabling. They can be built on optimism or pessimism. Our beliefs actually determine what we think we are and are not capable of.

We create our own belief systems based on the conclusions we draw from the experiences we have and the results we produce.

This is the primary reason why successful people can continue to be successful even in the face of overwhelming odds. When your efforts produce a desired result, you record it emotionally as a successful experience. When you combine several of these positive experiences you establish a pattern, a pattern of success.

Once you have established a pattern of success, you develop the emotional viewpoint of a successful person. This becomes your belief system. Because your actions have produced positive results in the past, you have every reason to believe that they will produce successful results in the future. This is an empowering belief system that will fill you with optimism and the courage to take on new challenges with confidence.

What if our efforts in the past have not produced the results we intended? What if several failed attempts have combined to form a limiting belief system rather than a successful one? Is there a way to change an unwanted belief system?

Yes and here's why; while personal experiences contribute to our beliefs, we need to keep in mind that there is always more than one way to interpret any situation. We have the ability to decide what value we will assign to any experience in our life. Each of us has the capacity to view even a negative experience as something valuable.

People often develop limiting beliefs because in the past they have been unable to achieve the results they wanted. When past efforts have led to pain instead of pleasure, it is easy to conclude that further efforts will just lead to more pain.

This type of mindset creates a negative reinforcement loop. With each painful experience, fear increases and commitment decreases. Consequently, a lack of commitment produces disappointing results that reinforce the limiting belief.

When this occurs in more than one area of our life, there is a danger that we may start viewing ourselves as destined to fail. This is an extremely unhealthy pattern of belief that can leave you feeling paralyzed and unable to act. Such a pattern of learned helplessness is not based on reality, but rather, an exaggerated emotional reaction to the pain of disappointment.

One effective way to break limiting beliefs is to choose an area in your life where you know you can take control. No matter who we are, there is always some area in our life where we feel a level of competence. Start by setting a reachable goal in that direction and then take action.

When you experience success, set another reachable goal in that same direction and follow through with more action. Continue this pattern until you become comfortable with your ability to produce your intended outcome.

Now you have created a positive reinforcement loop. Next, choose another area in your life where you have a degree of competence and repeat the process. As your feelings of confidence grow, allow yourself to identify with your success. Learn to view yourself as a successful person and attach feelings of approval to your positive experiences.

You can also explain your challenge to a friend and ask them to provide you with some positive feedback every time you succeed in producing an intended result. Now you will have both an external and an internal source of positive validation.

Creating a belief system that empowers you to confidently take action in the direction of your goals is a huge step in your personal development. Now, let's look at some ways to deal with limiting beliefs so that if you experience any disappointing results, you won't slip back into a negative mindset.

If limiting belief systems are preventing us from taking action, can we change them? Yes, and it's not as difficult as you might think. There are several steps involved in dismantling a negative belief. Let's go through them one at a time.

If we have adopted a limiting belief system we have probably done so out of fear. If past efforts have yielded painful results we may feel safer doing nothing. The desire to feel safe and secure has a powerful effect on our willingness to take action.

"When action represents risk and inaction represents safety, our built-in desire for security will severely limit our ability to act."

One way to move away from this mindset is to realize that our past does not equal our future. If we examine why past efforts did not lead to our intended result, we will likely discover that our approach was not as well thought-out as we may have believed.

Start by asking yourself the following questions:
   1) Did I skip or minimize essential steps?
   2) Did I fail to prepare before taking action?
   3) Did I truly understand what was needed?

The more you question your previous performance, the more likely you are to discover the source of your disappointing results. This will move your internal focus away from fear and toward identifying the problem and finding a solution.

There is a tendency to follow our beliefs without questioning them, but asking questions about a belief creates doubt. Once we introduce doubt into the equation, a negative belief loses much of its emotional power and becomes subject to reason. This helps us to see the need to make adjustments and to reevaluate our previous approach.

Another effective dismantling tool for a negative belief system is to link it to pain. What have been the long-term results of your limiting beliefs? Have you suffered emotionally, financially, or in some other way by clinging to those beliefs?

If you can identify ways that your old belief system has caused you pain in the past, and is likely to bring you pain in the future, you will be motivated to move away from it. The more you associate pain with your limiting beliefs, the easier it will be to change.

Once your old belief system is cloaked in doubt and pain, it is time to create a new one. At this point you will _want_ to change. Now change will come to represent pleasure, and you will feel ready to move toward pleasure and away from pain. Even though doubt and pain are considered negative emotions, they become useful success tools when attached to an unwanted belief. Remodeling any belief that limits us requires that we change the feelings (emotional anchors) that are linked to those beliefs.

A life spent in the pursuit of personal excellence will, from time to time, encounter disappointing results. The way we view those results and our ability to extract valuable lessons from them, will have an enormous impact on our level of success. It is quite possible to have a limiting belief system in place without even being aware of it. As individuals, it's absolutely vital that we carefully examine our own beliefs to make sure that they are empowering us rather than limiting us.

The following exercises are designed to do exactly that. After taking inventory of your current beliefs we will categorize them, examine their emotional anchors, and then make any necessary modifications.

It may sound complicated, I know, but don't worry about it. We are going to break the whole process down into several easy to manage steps. The first thing I want you to do is write down your beliefs about yourself and your abilities on two separate sheets of paper. On one sheet write the beliefs that empower you, on the other those that limit you.

Let's start with your empowering beliefs.

How do you view your own abilities? Any area in your life where you are producing good results is an area where you have empowering beliefs about your own abilities.

Let's take some time to examine and list those areas along with the beliefs and feelings that support them. These are some of your greatest personal assets. They are the beliefs that you want to support and strengthen. Answering the following questions will get you started.

1) What are you good at, and why do you think that is?
2) Which areas of your own life do you feel competent about, and why?
3) At what new activity do you think you would do well, and why do you think that?
4) What is your favorite activity, and why do you like it so much?
5) In what area would you like a chance to prove yourself and why would you do well?
6) How do you like to help others, and why are you able to help them?
7) When you want to make a good impression, what do you do, and why?

Example 1:

Answering question **#1** - What are you good at, and why do you think that is?

> I am good at taking complicated concepts and making them simple so that others can easily understand them.
>
> The reason I can do this is because my mind naturally breaks things down into a sequence of logical steps.

Example 2:

Answering question **#6** - What do you like to help others with, and why are you able to help them?

> I like to help others organize by packing a lot of stuff into a limited space like the trunk of a car or a storage unit.
>
> It's a strange talent but I'm good at it and others appreciate the help. The reason I can do this is a high mechanical aptitude. (Weird but true)

Okay, now it's your turn, list as many answers as you can to those seven questions. Include any area of your life where you feel some degree of competency, no matter how small or insignificant they might seem. Be sure to include the reason for each. .

If you take your time and really focus, I think you'll discover that there are actually a lot of things to put on your list. When you're done, I need you to go back and describe the positive emotions associated with each item on your list. Here's what I mean by that:

Going back to my first example, it makes me feel happy to help someone understand something. My positive emotional anchor for the first example is a feeling of happiness or joy. In the second example it's about giving, making a contribution to help others.

When you finish, you will have created a very significant personal development tool that will enable you to modify your limiting beliefs and unlock your hidden resources.

The part of your list we are most interested in is the reasons you listed for each item, and the feeling that goes with it. Those reasons represent your empowering beliefs. The feelings are the emotional anchors for those beliefs. Go back and highlight the reason and feeling for everything on your list. When you are done, prioritize them and list your top 7 on the next page following this format:

Activity: *Simplifying complicated concepts or tasks*
Belief: *I have the ability to break complex things down into a sequence of logical steps*
Feeling: *Happiness, Joy* (for example #1)

Empowering Beliefs about My Abilities

1) Activity: _____

   Belief: _____

   Feeling _____

2) Activity: _____

   Belief: _____

   Feeling _____

3) Activity: _____

   Belief: _____

   Feeling: _____

4) Activity: _____

   Belief: _____

   Feeling: _____

5) Activity: _____

   Belief: _____

   Feeling: _____

6) Activity: _____

   Belief: _____

   Feeling: _____

7) Activity: _____

   Belief: _____

   Feeling: _____

This list is a powerful resource for modifying your beliefs and transforming the quality of your life. Do not underestimate the value of being familiar with your empowering beliefs.

If you have more than seven or don't want to write them in your book, just use a separate sheet of paper. As time goes by, your list will grow. Be sure to keep it updated.

Let's examine and change your limiting beliefs. Are there areas in your life where you can't seem to produce the results you intend? Any area in your life where you are not producing good results is an area where you are holding onto limiting beliefs about your own abilities.

Now it's time to examine and list those areas, along with the beliefs and feelings that support them. These areas are currently emotional liabilities. They are the beliefs that limit you, and need to be changed. As in the last exercise, answering the following questions will get you started.

1) What do you feel you are not very good at, and why do you think that is so?
2) What areas of your life leave you feeling incompetent or unqualified and why?
3) What new activity are you afraid to try, but would like to? Why do you feel afraid?
4) What is your least favorite activity, and why do you dislike it so much?
5) In what area do you want to improve, and what do you feel is holding you back?
6) What do you avoid helping others with, and why do you feel unable to help them?
7) When you want to make a good impression, what do you try to hide, and why?

List as many answers as you can to the seven questions exactly the way you did in the last exercise. Include any area of your life that leaves you feeling limited, incompetent, unqualified or afraid. Be sure to include the reason for, and feelings behind each one.

I realize that this can be a difficult and even an uncomfortable exercise. It takes courage and honesty to face your limiting beliefs. I promise that you won't have to deal with the discomfort very long. Once you finish your list I will show you how to rid yourself of these emotional liabilities and replace them with more empowering beliefs. This list does not need to be overwhelming. If you need to, just do a few at a time, then come back and do a few more.

Follow the same format as before listing the activity, the belief and the feeling, but for now you should <u>leave the painful anchor line blank</u>.

Limiting Beliefs about My Abilities

1) Activity: _____

Belief: _____

Feeling: _____

Painful Anchor: _____

2) Activity: _____

Belief: _____

Feeling: _____

Painful Anchor: _____

3) Activity: _Going to places_____

Belief: _People judging, gossyping, and exploiting me_ *laughing*

Feeling: _Unhappiness, Fear, anxiety and stress___

Painful Anchor: _Rejection, inferior, insecurity, low confidence_

4) Activity: _____

Belief: _____

Feeling: _____

Painful Anchor: _____

5) Activity: _Being myself_

Belief: _thinking I am unworthy, un sincere_

Feeling: _Unhappiness fear, anxiety, depression_

Painful Anchor: _Rejection, fear_

6) Activity: _Kindness and Confidently speak to others_

Belief: _I think I am a poseur_

Feeling: _Unhappiness, Depression_

Painful Anchor: _Rejection, fear_

7) Activity: _____

Belief: _____

Feeling: _____

Painful Anchor: _____

This list will not be around very long. You are about to strip it of its power and break free of its influence for good. Once you learn these techniques, you will be able to quickly disable any belief that tries to limit you in the future.

To begin dismantling your limiting beliefs, you need to link them to a painful, negative, emotional anchor. The more painful the anchor, the more effective it will be.

Start by asking yourself some pointed questions about each belief such as:

1) What price have I paid because of this belief?

2) How is this belief affecting me financially, physically and emotionally?

3) Why did I get anchored in this limiting belief to begin with?

Continuing to question the validity and consequences of your limiting beliefs will create a negative feedback loop. Doing this will expose a wide array of negative emotional anchors for those beliefs. Once they come to represent pain, it becomes much easier to move away from them and move toward beliefs that represent pleasure.

Go through this process with all of your limiting beliefs and assign one or more painful emotional anchors to each one of them. Write them on your list on the line for painful anchor. Do this now to complete your list of limiting beliefs.

Next, ask yourself a few simple questions.

1) What would I have to believe in order to succeed in this area of my life?

2) What would I have to do differently in order to produce the results I want?

3) Which of my existing, empowering beliefs can I apply to these areas of my life?

Now, look at your list of empowering beliefs and read them out loud. This list represents some of your most powerful personal resources. By saying them out loud, you will unlock the answers to those three questions above. Write your answers down, and then read them out loud as well.

Allow yourself to develop a sense of certainty that, by changing your beliefs, you will be able to produce positive results. Now you have something pleasurable to move toward.

The beliefs you have will determine the actions you take. By examining your current belief systems you can consistently choose beliefs that will empower you to act.

What kind of beliefs are truly empowering? Which ones help us to reach our goals and succeed in improving the quality of our life? The answer is simple really, beliefs that empower us to take action and make positive changes. This would include beliefs that move us toward a positive perception of events and circumstances, while encouraging us to modify our behavior accordingly.

Feelings and behavior define who we are as a person. Most of the time our behavior is just the outward manifestation of our feelings, and our feelings are a reflection of how we view things through the window of our beliefs.

Is the glass half full or half empty? Was that person trying to insult me or are they just running low on resources? Does this challenge represent a negative experience or an opportunity? The answers really depend upon your beliefs and how you choose to sort information and view circumstances.

If we are empowered by our beliefs, then we will have an optimistic feeling about the first question, an empathetic view of the other person in the second question, and think of possibilities in regard to the third question. Both our feelings and our behavior, in relation to these three questions will demonstrate that our beliefs actually empower us.

Patterning

One of the easiest ways to move your beliefs in a more positive direction is to use a process called patterning. This is a technique where we change our behavior to produce a positive effect on our feelings.

As our feelings become more positive so do our beliefs. Behavior includes our speech, body language and physical bearing.

Here's an example of how I have used this simple technique in my own life with great results. Years ago when people would ask me: "How are you?" I thought it was humorous to answer, "Pretty good for an old guy." One day, I finally stopped to consider the consequences that reply was having on my nervous system. I quickly realized that I could actually be programming myself for premature aging. All that my subconscious was hearing was, "You're OLD." So I changed.

Now when someone asks me how I am, my standard reply is, "absolutely fantastic." Every time I use that reply I reinforce my internal viewpoint about how I feel. So, how do I really feel? The truth is that I really do feel   fantastic.

Normally, our feelings are a reflection of our beliefs and our behavior is a reflection of our feelings. So, I chose to reverse this process. I conditioned my feelings and my beliefs using my behavior.

This is actually a very simple process with its scientific basis in quantum physics. The words we use create a vibration that directly affects our thoughts and feelings. If we continue to generate that vibration, our internal programming will rearrange itself accordingly.

I encourage you to try this simple technique in any area of your life. Use empowering words, body language, thoughts, and physical bearing, to encourage the development of empowering beliefs. It's easy, it's fun, and you can start immediately.

Let's say you want to build your level of self-confidence. Simply adopt the external characteristics of someone with a great deal of confidence. If you walk, talk, dress and conduct yourself like a person who is very confident, you will send signals to your own nervous system that say, "I can do just about anything." You will also send those same messages to everyone you come in contact with. This will completely change the way they respond to you. Their response will add credibility to your newfound confidence.

Actors call this getting "in character." In their minds they become the person they are trying to represent. I encourage you to use this same technique to represent the person you want to become. It will reprogram your beliefs about yourself and your abilities.

> "If I have the belief that I can do it, I shall surely acquire the capacity to do it even if I may not have it at the beginning." - Mahatma Ghandi

There are actually several ways to work with our beliefs in order to improve the quality of our lives. The following method is designed to precondition your nervous system so it will readily accept a new belief of your choosing.

Pacing and Leading

The concept here is that we can use what we already believe as an anchor to encourage the acceptance of a new, empowering belief.

For instance, most of us know that flipping a switch on the wall will control whether the light is on or off. That's a belief based on a fact. We also believe that turning the key in the ignition of a car will start the engine. These are established beliefs that we know will produce the intended result.

Here is a way that you can use your current, proven beliefs to condition your nervous system to accept a new belief. It gives instant, positive reinforcement to new beliefs that you want to adopt by using the principles of association or transference.

This technique uses what is called <u>pacing and leading</u> statements, developed by Richard Bandler and John Grinder, the co-founders of NLP (*Neuro-Linguistic Programming*). While some use this process to try and influence others, our interest is in self-application.

You start by pacing or affirming things that you already believe are true, such as:

- My name is _____
- I live _____
- I am _____ years old.
- 2+2=4
- The switch controls the light.
- The key starts the car.

By pacing with your current beliefs, you are creating momentum that will carry over to your new belief. The certainty of your established beliefs will be transferred to your new belief because it will become linked to the same established sense of credibility.

Your mind will accept it as part of the same group and attach the same certainty to it.

Here is an example of the process:

- My name is _____ (pacing)
- I live _____ (pacing)
- I am_____ years old. (pacing)
- 2+2=4. (pacing)
- The switch controls the light. (pacing)
- The key starts the car. (pacing)
- ▶ My life is noticeably better every day. (leading)

It is recommended that you use between four and seven established beliefs to pace your new belief. This will create enough credibility to anchor the new belief.

If you could measure the strength of your new belief, "my life is noticeably better every day," here is what you would find; before you start this process, that belief would be rather weak.

By the time you have repeated the process several times your level of belief in the new statement would be much stronger. Each time you repeat the sequence, the new belief is strengthened until you reach the point where you subconsciously accept it as fact.

"In any project the important factor is your belief.
Without belief there can be no successful outcome."
-William James

Once your mind accepts it as a fact, you will no longer question the new belief. Consequently, your behavior will change and your world will begin to reflect the positive results of your new belief. What will the effect be? Your life will actually become noticeably better each and every day.

Here's an important key to making this work; for your new belief to be able to exert a powerful influence on your life, it needs to be anchored in emotions. This can work two ways; use positive emotions to anchor a constructive belief, or use negative emotions to associate pain with an unwanted belief.

Adding the Emotional Component

Now, let's go back to our example: "My life is noticeably better every day." In order to multiply the positive effect of this new belief in our life it needs an emotional anchor. In our last exercise of pacing and leading, we paced our new belief with non-emotional beliefs that we knew to be true.

This time we want to transfer the positive emotional value of beliefs that already bring us pleasure.

Here's an example of how that might look once we add a positive emotional component.

- I love to vacation in Hawaii. (pacing)
- There's nothing as beautiful as a sunset on the ocean. (pacing)
- My favorite restaurant is_____ (pacing)
- Rumba music makes me want to dance. (pacing)
- The sound of the ocean is so peaceful. (pacing)
- ▶ I love the way my life is noticeably better every single day. (leading)

Using this method will cause the positive, emotional value of the first five beliefs to be transferred to your new belief. You can reinforce this new belief by simply closing your eyes and allowing yourself to experience all of the positive emotions attached to these five pacing statements. Doing this regularly will attach the same powerful, positive, emotional anchors to your new belief.

The belief that your life is getting noticeably better every day will trigger all of the wonderful emotions you have already attached to the other five beliefs. This kind of thinking will radically alter how you feel about, and approach, each new day.

Have you ever noticed how good you feel when you wake up in the morning knowing that you have something really wonderful to look forward to that day? If you are getting on a plane tomorrow for a long deserved vacation in Hawaii, you will likely wake up energized and full of eager anticipation. By using this method you can actually capture those same feelings every day.

Our beliefs always exert a very powerful force on our physical and emotional states. Understanding this concept gives you an amazingly simple yet effective way to establish control over your personal belief systems.

You can also use this same process to disable beliefs that bring you short-term pleasure but cause pain in the long run. Imagine that you have a problem overindulging in desserts. How could you use this process to overcome that problem? The reason you enjoy desserts so much is that you have linked them to a pleasurable anchor.

The goal is to remove the positive, emotional anchor

and replace it with a negative one. Let's see how that might look when we add a negative, emotional component.

- Every time I overeat I get disgusted with myself. (pacing)
- I feel really sad that I can't fit into my favorite clothes anymore. (pacing)
- The more I eat, the less energy I have. (pacing)
- My doctor says I'm pre-diabetic and that scares me. (pacing)
- ▶ The sight of chocolate cake makes me sick. (leading)

For this to work, you need to pace your new belief with current beliefs that have a very strong, negative, emotional anchor.

Note: The ones I used are kind of light duty, but for your own purposes use the most painful ones you can think of. By the time you reach your new belief you want to be feeling so disgusted that it actually hurts to think about it.

> "Arguing *for* negative thinking under certain circumstances is very different from arguing against positive thinking." -Julie Norem

Keep in mind that everything we do in life is motivated by pain or pleasure. We are either moving toward pleasure, away from pain, or both. It's up to you to decide which beliefs will be anchored in pain, and which beliefs will be anchored in pleasure.

Creative Daydreaming

Another process that you can use to help reshape your beliefs is creative daydreaming. Simply spend time consistently daydreaming about the life you desire to live.

Each time you do this your mind becomes more receptive to the idea until it begins to view the new possibility as a reality. This is the basis for the creative visualization process. In reality, visualization doesn't actually change anything, except your beliefs. In turn, the new beliefs move you to take action and create the desired changes.

You can take this process one step further and project it out into the world around you by simply pretending that things are the way you would like them to be. Have you ever heard the expression, "Fake it till you make it"? Children have a wonderful and seemingly uninhibited ability to pretend. As it turns out, this is a powerful process for initiating behavioral modification.

The bottom line is this: Your world will reflect your beliefs in the experiences you have. Our beliefs tend to act like a powerful magnet that attracts supporting experiences into our lives. Once you alter your beliefs, your experiences will change correspondingly.

By controlling your beliefs you control your reality.

"Don't limit yourself. Many people limit themselves to what they think they can do. You can go as far as your mind lets you. What you believe, remember, you can achieve." -Mary Kay Ash

---

Congratulations! This section is a lot of work and you should feel really good about what you've accomplished. Now that you have the tools to initiate a transformation, let's go see how to use them.

Section Review

In the first chapter we discussed the value of internal harmony as a basis for inner peace and happiness.

Have you identified areas of internal conflict?

In Chapter 2 we talked about your personal values and the importance of having a set of guiding principles.

Have you created your list of 3-5 guiding principles?

Next, we learned that we all move toward pleasure and away from pain according to our emotional anchors.

Have you started deciding for yourself what represents pain and what represents pleasure?

Learning to master your passions is one of the very first steps toward mastering your life.

Did you list your top ten passions?

Established response patterns constantly influence us.

Were you able to identify with any of the examples?

Beliefs can be empowering or limiting. Some are assets and some are liabilities.

Did you discover your empowering beliefs and feelings?

Did you identify your limiting beliefs and assign a painful emotional anchor to each of them?

Have you used the dismantling techniques to break free from the influence of your limiting beliefs?

Section 2 - Motive Connection

Make It Personal

About Section 2

The motive connection is designed to help you discover a number of things about your relationship with the concept of personal success.

There are no written exercises for you to do. There are, however, a number of viewpoint questions that will help you to get very clear about what you want to accomplish in your life and why.

Success means different things to different people. You need to understand what it means to you so that you don't end up chasing someone else's dream. One of the primary ways to guarantee that your achievements bring you a sense of joy and satisfaction is to uncover your personal version of success and the motives behind it.

As you go through this section, try to disassociate yourself with your current ideas about what you think you want. Stay open to self-discovery and see what unfolds!

Chapters 7-9

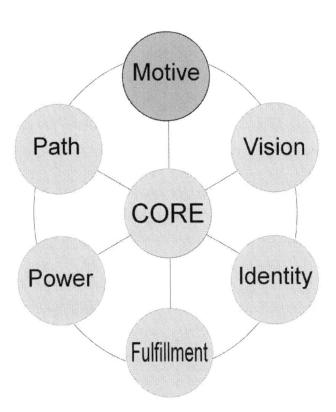

Chapter 7 -

What is Success?

Success is one of those concepts that we all understand, and yet, in reality it means something different to each individual. What might represent financial abundance to you might represent poverty to someone like Donald Trump.

Your concept of being physically fit is probably not the same as that of an elite Olympic athlete. While swimming a quarter of a mile might represent your new personal best, to someone about to swim the English Channel it doesn't mean much.

The point is this; in order to be successful in any endeavor, you must first identify what success means to you personally. Some people are just looking for success in one specific area of life, such as relationships or business.

Keep in mind that it is entirely possible to be very successful in one area of life and still be struggling in other areas. For many successful people this is exactly the situation they find themselves in.

> "Never mind what others do; do better than yourself, beat your own record from day to day and you are a success." -H. Boetcker

Sometimes people choose to make a conscious trade-off, neglecting one or more aspects of their life in order to succeed in another. For example, workaholics don't generally have the most meaningful family lives. Everyone at work may see them as a total success, while their families are likely to feel quite differently.

So when we think of living a successful life, we are really talking about having a reasonable measure of success in many different areas of our life. For that to be a reality, it's absolutely vital that we establish a definition for success in each of those areas. This is the only way that we can gauge our progress.

For our purposes, let's define success as *achieving your intended outcomes*. This definition makes it clear that success does not happen by accident. In order to be successful in any area, we must first decide upon an intended result or outcome. Doing so will allow us to know where we are going, and what to expect when we get there. This definition also helps us to measure our success according to our own standards, not someone else's.

People tend to measure success by the results that they can see. Sadly, many people consider material wealth as the most accurate indicator of success. A person of modest means might be a wonderful husband and father, well liked and appreciated by everyone that knows him, but still not considered successful. On the flip side, a very wealthy person might make those around him feel horrible, and yet he is still viewed as a successful person.

> "What's money? A man is a success if he gets up in the morning and goes to bed at night and in between does what he wants to do."
> -Bob Dylan

It's also possible to be very successful in certain areas of your life, and not even recognize it. Have you ever heard someone say, "I never knew what I had until I lost it"? That statement immediately makes us think of somebody who had a good relationship and then threw it away. In other words, they had a successful relationship but failed to recognize it. If they had established a clear set of criteria for identifying a successful relationship, this would never have happened.

All these examples help us to fully appreciate why it is

so important to ask ourselves, "What does success really mean to me?" Overall success requires asking yourself this question with regard to your relationships, finances, physical condition, and anything else that's important to you.

Realize that <u>successful</u> is not something that we do, it is something we become. First, we become successful in our minds, and then we can become successful on the outside.

A successful person isn't that way because of what they have accomplished. Their view of themselves is not dependent on their external achievements. They already see themselves as successful; it's part of their identity. We call this a successful mindset. External accomplishments are the natural outgrowth of a successful mindset.

Many of the greatest achievers in history have succeeded in spite of numerous setbacks. For example, in 1878 Thomas Edison boldly announced to the world that he would invent an inexpensive electric light that would replace the gaslight. Often ridiculed, Edison tried over ten thousand different experiments before he finally presented the world with the first incandescent light bulb on October 21, 1879.

Do you think that Thomas Edison ever saw himself as a failure during that time period? This is what he had to say in the face of ridicule, "I didn't fail ten thousand times. I successfully eliminated ten thousand combinations which wouldn't work." Thomas Edison had a successful mindset, and eventually he found a way to produce his intended result.

So, in Thomas Edison we see a perfect example of a successful mindset. Even when he did not produce the results he intended he did not see it as a failure. He had a clear picture of what success would mean, and he constantly took action toward that end.

He was not daunted by the fact that he didn't produce his intended result quickly. As far as he was concerned, eliminating what didn't work was just part of the process that led to his eventual success.

Experiencing greater success in every important aspect of your life can start here and now. Obviously, you want to develop the same type of successful mindset as we've been talking about. To help you do that, there are a couple more things that we need to consider.

Whenever we want to accomplish something, being aware of our deeper motives is an important key to being successful. To discover what your motives are, you must...

Chapter 8 -

Always Ask Why?

Asking ourselves 'why' we want to succeed at something is a powerful way of getting a clear picture of our own motives. It allows us to discover underlying desires, and expand our awareness of purpose.

'Why' seems like such a simple question, after all, two-year-olds can ask it all day long. But when we carefully examine the 'why' behind our desire to succeed, we usually learn things about ourselves that we were not aware of.

Knowing why we want to accomplish something helps us identify the feelings we expect to experience once we get there. If we know what success will feel like, then we know where we are going emotionally. Remember, success starts on the inside.

Let's use a desire for financial success as an example. Almost without exception, people want to be financially successful. In our society, the terms successful and financially successful are basically synonymous.

Countless millions live under the assumption that

money equals freedom, happiness, and fulfillment. In other words, money is the key to the life of their dreams.

So, emotionally speaking, financial success comes to represent every good feeling that people want to experience to a greater degree. On an emotional level, money comes to represent the path to a happier, more meaningful life. Is it any wonder that achieving financial success tends to be a hollow victory for most?

Is there anything wrong with having money? No, not as long as we understand ahead of time that money only solves financial problems. Money is a material resource, not a ticket to emotional fulfillment.

Asking ourselves why we want to achieve financial success provides an opportunity to identify unrealistic expectations. By eliminating inappropriate emotional anchors, we will be able to get clear on what financial success actually represents, and what we can realistically expect it to feel like.

Knowing ahead of time what success will actually feel like enables us to do two important things.

1) It makes it possible to identify success once we achieve it.
2) You don't need to wait to feel successful. You can begin immediately.

Why would you wait to feel successful once you have identified what it will feel like?

Success begins on the inside. It's a state of mind with a strong emotional anchor. Your feelings are a huge part of your identity. If you allow yourself to feel successful, you will see yourself as a successful person. As a result, you will adopt the thinking patterns that will motivate you to take action and produce results.

Keep in mind that producing your intended result does not, in and of itself, make you a successful person. It does however, provide some confirmation. Results do provide external evidence of a successful mindset. However, the lack of immediate results does not mean that you are not a successful person.

Remember, Thomas Edison was a successful person who produced his intended result, but only after 10,000 attempts. If he had allowed those attempts to determine his identity, he would have viewed himself as a failure.

Instead of changing his successful mindset, he used those failed attempts to help him make adjustments in the way he took action. Every time he produced the wrong result, he used that information to adjust his approach. And as they say, the rest is history.

The point to take away from this is → you have the ability to adopt the mindset and emotional anchors of a successful person. It is a choice that you can make. Never allow circumstances, lack of desired results, or the opinions of others, to make that choice for you. Never forget that success is first and foremost a state of mind.

Maybe we want to be more successful in the way we relate to other people. Perhaps, we want to be a happier person. Maybe we've decided to improve our physical or emotional condition. No matter what area of life we are talking about, the principles remain the same.

As we continue to explore 'why' we want to be financially successful, what else should we consider? We have already determined that money is just a material resource. On its own, it has no effect on our pain or pleasure paradigms. It is the emotional anchors we attach to money that will determine its effect.

To become financially successful, we need to link having money to a <u>realistic</u> and positive emotional anchor. It needs to represent a <u>legitimate</u> source of pleasure that we can move toward. Likewise, we want to link the lack of money to a negative feeling that we will move away from. This brings us back to asking <u>why</u> we want the money.

Creating a legitimate and realistic positive anchor is as easy as filling in two blank lines. **But before you do that, please read the next four paragraphs.**

On the positive side, $_____ a month will allow me to meet all my obligations with enough left over for_____

_____

Whatever you decide to put in the second space should represent emotional pleasure. It might be a single thing like a vacation with someone you love, or it might be a list of several things. What is most important here is that your answer has emotional value; there must be feelings, preferably strong feelings, attached to it.

There are two things I want you to verify before you decide on a positive emotional anchor for having money. Go back to your list of 3-5 *guiding principles for internal harmony* that you created in the chapter on Personal Values. Make sure that the choice you make now is in harmony with those principles. If not, find another anchor for having money. Do not compromise your principles if you want to succeed.

Next, go back and look at your list of *Top 10 Passions* that you created in the section on Choosing Your Passions. You already know that you can get excited about these things. This list represents your most powerful, positive, emotional anchors. Now you have an opportunity to put it to use.

By working within the protective boundaries of your guiding principles, and utilizing the energy of your passions, you have created a powerful motivation for success. Instead of unrealistic expectations, your reasons for wanting money are ethical, realistic and passionate. *Now, go back and create your positive emotional anchor for money.*

Asking why has allowed you to define a pleasurable emotional association for financial success. The more you visit these feelings, the greater their influence on your financial prosperity. Once these feelings become part of your belief system you will be a financially successful person on the inside. It will become who you are, and sooner or later, it will manifest externally. When that happens, it will feel natural because it will resonate with your emotional identity.

This process might sound long and drawn out, but it can happen very fast. In less than two years Edison transformed the way the world made light. Imagine how quickly that change would have occurred if he had only needed 50 attempts instead of 10,000.

Now it is time to create a springboard, just in case you get off course. Think about what the lack of money represents to you, and why you want to avoid that situation. Most people have no problem with this one. All you need to do is isolate one painful consequence of not having any money. If you can't think of one from a personal experience, use one from someone else's life. Take a daytime drive through a really poor neighborhood. Have a close look at someone who lives on the street. You don't have to go far to see the pain and suffering that poverty can bring.

Imagining yourself in a similar situation can create a very painful negative anchor. If moving toward pleasure ever requires a little boost, moving away from the pain associated with that image should do the trick.

> When we think of personal success there is one very important aspect that is easily overlooked. Our motives should embrace the big picture. For that to happen, we really need to...

Chapter 9 -

Think Beyond Yourself

There is one more aspect to consider when designing success in any given area of your life. This is so important that it can multiply your sense of satisfaction by a factor of a thousand or more.

Here it is. Always think beyond yourself. Design your successes to benefit others, as well as yourself. Create value that reaches beyond your needs and desires, and touches the lives of others in a positive way.

When your efforts contribute to the lives of other people, you will discover the deep joy of giving. If you design your pursuit of success with this in mind, great and wonderful things will begin to happen on a daily basis.

We live in a world that is increasingly self-serving. Nobody benefits from this mentality. Selfish ambitions produce hollow results. Perhaps the most damaging fraud ever perpetrated on the human family is the lie that selfishness is necessary, or that it leads to anything of value.

Today's world is a sad reminder of the consequences produced by relentless greedy pursuits. I challenge you to reject the mindset of competition, and instead, embrace one of contribution. If you look for ways to enrich the lives of others, you will begin to experience success on a level far beyond the comprehension of most.

"It is one of the most beautiful compensations of life, that no man can sincerely try to help another without helping himself." -Ralph Waldo Emerson

Always consider how the pursuit of your goals will affect those around you. Never underestimate one person's potential to have a positive impact on the lives of countless others.

If you seek opportunities to contribute, your world will expand in unimaginable ways. You will become the beneficiary of your own contributions. How can you do this?

Maybe your current circumstances don't seem to support such a possibility. This does not limit your ability to add value to the lives of others. Do what you can and watch as your world expands before you.

Could you make it a goal to smile at everyone who makes eye contact with you? Do you have opportunities to sincerely commend others? How do you feel when people smile at you or commend you? Doesn't that contribute to the quality of your life?

Would it be possible for you to take five minutes each day to connect with someone else on a personal level? Most of us want to contribute in this way, but may not be making the time to do so. Could you set a goal to start making the time?

"Three billion people on the face of the earth go to bed hungry every night, but four billion people go to bed every night hungry for a simple word of encouragement and recognition." -Cavett Robert

You have already learned some powerful skills from reading this book and doing the exercises in it. Is there someone in need that you could share these things with? You may be very pleasantly surprised at the positive impact you can have on others.

Recently, I spent a few minutes talking with a lady who had developed a paralyzing fear of crowds. At one time in her life, she had been an outgoing and adventurous truck driver. Now she struggles just to go into the market. Every time I steered the conversation back to her truck driving days I noticed that she would perk up a bit.

Finally, I asked her to tell me what it felt like to hit the open road in that big truck early in the morning just as the sun was coming up, before there was any traffic. As she changed her focus to access those memories, her whole physiology changed. She sat up straighter, became more alert. After thinking about it for a moment, she looked me in the eyes and smiled as she said, "powerful." Suddenly, she was a different person.

I explained that she could access those feelings anytime she wanted to. All she needed to do was sit up straight like she was now, and feel herself behind the wheel of that big truck. You could tell by the look on her face that she hadn't felt that good in years. And, she was truly grateful for the relief that she was experiencing.

Was she the only one to benefit? No, not at all. I also experienced an incredible amount of joy from our short conversation. That experience literally made my day. It was a total win-win situation. All because I took a few minutes to talk to someone I barely knew.

You already know enough about human behavior and belief systems to do the same thing. It's not difficult. All you have to do is actively look for opportunities to contribute.

If you use the same process we just applied to creating financial success, you can easily create a successful contributor's mindset. Remember, it all starts with the person we choose to become on the inside, our emotional identity. I encourage you to openly embrace the identity of a contributor and experience the deep joy of giving.

"Whatever you think the world is withholding from you, you are withholding from the world."

~

"Whatever you think people are withholding from you -praise, appreciation, assistance, loving care, and so on, give it to them."

~

"You cannot receive what you don't give. Outflow determines inflow." -Eckhart Tolle

Congratulations. The groundwork has been laid. Now it's time to make things happen.

Section Review

In this section we examined how important it is to identify what success really means to you personally.

Have you given it some thought?

We compared the difference between success on a monetary level, and a truly successful life.

Which one do you want?

True success starts with our mindset, the way we view ourselves and the results we produce.

Are you ready to see yourself as a successful person?

Asking <u>why</u> we want to accomplish something helps us to sort out the motives and feelings behind our goals.

Have you figured out the <u>why</u> behind your goals yet?

Finally, we considered the value of creating success with the ability to touch the lives of others.

Can you identify with the role of a contributor?

Section 3 - Vision Connection

Intended Outcome

About Section 3

In this section we will examine how connecting your vision to well-defined goals can give you a 97% chance of achieving your intended outcome. We will also clear up some common misconceptions that, if not addressed, can easily lead you down the road to massive disappointment.

False starts and backtracking can destroy your momentum. Now is the time to make sure that you are not vulnerable. Many people operate from a mindset of scarcity and lack. Instead of solutions and possibilities, they see limits. Let's make sure that's not you.

Anticipating possible roadblocks to your progress is a very effective way to avoid potential problems. When we fail to prepare we are just inviting problems.

Chapters 10-13

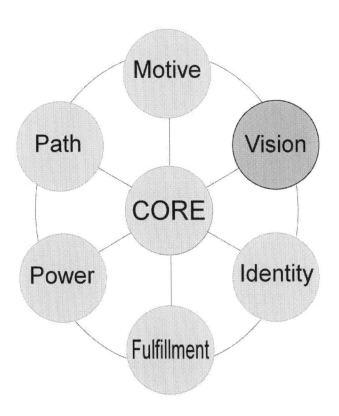

Chapter 10 -

Clearly Defined Goals

Many years ago, in what has come to be a highly publicized study, a group of researchers interviewed the graduating class of a well-known Ivy League University. They asked each graduate if they had established clearly defined goals for their future and if they had written them down. Remarkably, only 3% said yes to this question.

Think about that for a moment. These were all intelligent college graduates. They were all young, full of energy and ready to make their mark on the world as they carved out a meaningful future for themselves.

Even so, only 3% realized the value of having clearly defined goals. Evidently, the expensive and demanding education received by the entire group failed to adequately teach the true value and power of goal setting. The shortsightedness of their curriculum becomes even more obvious when we evaluate how things turned out over time.

The researchers tracked all the graduates for twenty years. Now that's plenty of time to allow for a variety of circumstances and obstacles to affect the entire group, including the ones who had established their goals at graduation. At the end of the twenty years, the 3% had a combined net worth greater than the other 97% put together.

This is a striking testimony to the power of goal setting. One of the key factors here is that those in the successful group did not just have vague goals floating around in the back of their minds. They were well defined and written down.

"Nothing can stop the man with the right mental attitude from achieving his goal; nothing on earth can help the man with the wrong mental attitude"
-Thomas Jefferson

Here's a more current statistic. It is estimated that about 97% of the people who set out to make money on the Internet fail to generate even a small monthly income.

In stark contrast, the other 3% earn anywhere from $10,000 - $100,000 per month and more.

Do you see a trend here?

No doubt everyone who has started a business on the Internet had the goal of making money. But did they have a clearly defined goal? Did they have a strategy for achieving their goal? Were they totally committed to producing their intended outcome? We know that for roughly 3%, the answer is yes.

Without a clearly defined goal, our chances of success in any major pursuit are likely to plummet to an unacceptable level. Achieving goals is a learned skill that follows a specific process.

One of my goals is to present those specifics in a way that makes it easy for you to achieve your goals, and improve the quality of your life.

Both of these examples focus on income because when we are talking about money it is easy to illustrate the value of having clearly defined goals. However, the power of goal setting applies to every aspect of your life and reaches far beyond the boundaries of financial success.

Done correctly, we can use this same power to bring about positive changes in every area of life. Goal setting is an extremely valuable personal growth tool.

You can tailor goals to improve your productivity, reduce body weight, further your education, raise energy levels, improve your ability to communicate with others, supercharge the quality of personal relationships, develop better parenting skills and just about anything else you can think of.

From this list it's easy to see that the quality of your life and your personal sense of accomplishment is dramatically affected by the ability to set clearly defined goals. The skills involved in setting reachable goals and seeing them through to completion are not difficult. Still, there is a right way and a wrong way to go about it. Do it right and you can expect your rate of success to skyrocket.

> Understanding what constitutes a legitimate, reachable goal is something we need to clear up right now!

Chapter 11 -

Wants & Intentions

Many people are convinced that the driving force with the power to propel them toward achieving their goals is having a burning want or desire. We have all heard phrases such as "you need a burning desire" or "you've got to really want it."

Let's examine the dynamics of "**want**" and "**desire**" to see if such feelings are, in actuality, productive or counterproductive. The dictionary defines **want** like this: to be deficient; having a need; being in a state of neediness or poverty. To be lacking. The definition for the word **desire** is: to wish for; long for; crave; want.

Simply put, wanting is the awareness of not having or of lacking something. Desiring expresses a need to fill the void created by the want. So, wanting and desiring arise from the emotional discomfort or pain of not having. Because we move away from pain, we feel the need to fill the void caused by this painful lacking sensation.

Here's the problem. Every time we say, "**I want some- thing**" in our mind it is the same as saying "**I don't**

have something." This is not a thought or feeling that focuses on the solution, is it? In reality, thinking about what we don't have puts our focus squarely on the problem. In fact, it reinforces the problem. Every time we reinforce a problem, we detour ourselves from finding a solution.

So how do we turn things around so we are focused on the solution?

We simply hold an "intention" instead of a "want" or "desire." Even though we often use these three words interchangeably, the meaning of intention is quite different.

Here is what the dictionary has to say about **intention:** an act or instance of determining mentally upon some action or result; purpose or attitude toward; the effect of one's actions or conduct.

And of course the word **intention** is derived from the word **intent**, which means **"having the mind or will fixed on a goal."**

See the difference? <u>An intention focuses our energy on the solution, not the problem.</u>

"A good intention clothes itself with power"
-Ralph Waldo Emerson

Intentions are positive, proactive thought patterns capable of moving us away from the pain of wanting, toward the joy of having. Intentions give us purpose and direction. They help to align our focus and energy toward the fulfillment of our goals.

Once we consider how the mind actually process information we gain a greater appreciation for the importance of using the right terminology. Words and thoughts send signals to our nervous system. We want to make absolutely sure we're sending the right signals.

Once we realize that the mind is only creative, it becomes very clear why we must direct our thoughts, emotions, and energies toward solutions instead of problems.

This creative nature of the mind means that it creates whatever we focus on. If we focus on lack, the mind creates more lack. Conversely, when we focus on a solution, we give our mind a new creative direction.

What do we learn from this?

It is not about having or not having. I'm sure we can all make a list of things that we would like to have. Maybe you'd like to have more money, a happier marriage, a higher level of physical fitness or any number of other things. There is absolutely nothing wrong with having it all. But you can't get there by holding onto lack.

Wanting and desiring do not represent the pathway to having. It is in fact, a sure path to not having because you will create more of what you are focused on. Focus on scarcity and you create scarcity, focus on abundance and you create abundance.

Unlike wanting, an intention will motivate you to take action in the direction of a solution. This is because you are focused on the outcome, not the problem. When you let go of wanting, you actually open the door to having.

Does this mean that I always use the word intention instead of saying that I want or I desire something? No, not at all because language patterns have been deeply ingrained in us since childhood. Additionally, in many cases these terms really are interchangeable.

But when I am setting a goal, or looking for a solution to a problem, I try not to send mixed signals to my subconscious mind. There is a big difference between a common every day conversation and a situation where you are actively programming your mind to achieve results.

For example, when responding to a waitress who asks, "Would like a white or a wheat roll with your dinner?" Saying, "I want the wheat" is a perfectly normal response. Besides, the truth is you are lacking a roll, the solution is right there in front of you, and you want it.

Of course, you could just say "the wheat please" and leave the want out of your conversation altogether. This will help retrain your linguistic patterning.

The important point is: when you sit down to write out your goals, you need to use language that will move you in the direction of your intended outcome or result. Remember, the word intent literally means "to have your mind fixed on a goal." Real goal setting always leads to taking action. Intent and intention are both action words; consequently, they require us to take action.

Now that we understand that wanting and desiring do not lead to having, there's another distinction we need to consider briefly.

Chapter 12 -

Trying vs. Committing

I have known so many people who believe they have made a decision when they say they are going to try to do something.

Maybe they are going to try to lose some weight or try to start exercising. How many times have we all said, "I'm really going to try to_____"

What's wrong with this approach?

Using the word "try" implies a halfhearted effort at best. It sends the signal, "total lack of commitment." Saying you're going to "try", leaves the door wide open for failure, and in fact, it invites failure.

Your mind will form a link between try and fail, as in "I tried but failed."

"If you deny yourself commitment, what can you do with your life?" -Harvey Fierstein

Case in point: Which of these two statements sounds more convincing to you?

1) I am going to try to lose some weight.
2) First thing tomorrow, I am starting my diet and exercise program. I am totally committed to losing <u>twenty pounds</u> over the next <u>six weeks</u>, no matter what.

In the first example there will be little, if any positive results because there is no plan or strategy, no decisive moment, and no commitment. It is just wishful thinking, well intentioned, but wishful thinking nonetheless.

> "Commitment unlocks the doors of imagination, allows vision, and gives us the right stuff' to turn our dreams into reality" -James Womack

We will cover this subject in detail in Section 5 – Harness the Power. But, I wanted to touch on it briefly at this point so that you avoid the "try trap" right from the start. It is absolutely vital to realize that consistently producing results requires commitment.

Chapter 13 -

Overcoming Roadblocks

The body has a built-in program called homeostasis. The purpose of this program is to maintain the status quo. Here's how it affects you in a physical way.

Let's say you want to lose 20 pounds so you start a diet and exercise program. At first your efforts are producing good results and it seems like you will meet your goal without too much difficulty. But for some reason, the closer you get to your goal, the more effort is required for you to continue losing weight.

Why does the last 5 pounds require more effort than the first 15 pounds did?

In a word: <u>Homeostasis</u>.

The further away you get from your old "normal" weight, the harder homeostasis works to resist the change. Your body has what is called an established "set point" that is 20 pounds heavier than your new, intended weight. Homeostasis tries to prevent further weight loss in an effort to return to normal.

The only way to overcome the influence of this powerful internal program is to establish a new set point at your desired weight. Once that happens, homeostasis will begin to work for you instead of against you. This means that it will work to maintain your new weight even if you give in to temptation or miss some workouts. The same program that made it difficult for you to lose weight will now try to prevent you from gaining weight.

So when you begin to make a change, homeostasis provides resistance against your efforts. Once you establish and maintain a new standard, it works in your favor.

Here's the kicker. It takes time to establish a new set point. In fact it takes two years. That means you need to keep yourself at your new weight for two years before homeostasis will consider that to be your 'normal weight'.

Why am I bringing this up? There are two reasons. The first reason is that a large percentage of people who read this book have encountered this problem. If you have ever lost weight only to gradually gain it all back again, now you can understand why. If losing weight is one of the reasons you got this book, then you need to know what you're up against.

By the way, the transition from one set point to another is progressive. What does this mean? It means that after six months it gets easier. After one year it gets much easier, and so on.

Now, here's the second reason. You have an emotional program that we could call emotional homeostasis, and it has many of the very same characteristics as the physical version.

Whether you like your current belief systems and response patterns or not, the fact is, they are well established and likely to resist any efforts to change. But, as you establish a new emotional set point, this resistance will evaporate. The good news is that unlike physical change, emotional change can occur almost instantly.

What usually happens when you want to adopt a new mindset or belief system? Everything tends to work well as long as you are making a conscious effort. But, as soon as you shift your focus, or something goes wrong, you can easily slip into your old patterns.

To effectively change our beliefs, and thus our mindset, requires a dual effort. Adopting a new belief system is vital, but it is not enough to completely counteract an unwanted, established response pattern. These patterns represent our emotional set point. Their function is to maintain the status quo. They are anchored in limiting beliefs that must be dismantled if you are going to affect lasting change.

The problem is that sometimes these response patterns are so subtle that we can be completely unaware of their existence. For clarity on this type of response pattern, you can review the four examples at the end of chapter 5 - Response Patterns.

If you suspect that one or more of these forces are at work in your life, don't be overly concerned. We all have these patterns running on a subconscious level. Contrary to what some therapists would have you believe, we don't need to delve into the underlying reasons for such patterns.

Those patterns are anchored in limiting beliefs that we can dismantle. Some common manifestations of such beliefs include:

- Fear of change (It's not worth the risk)
- Lack of confidence (I can't do it)
- Low self-esteem (I'm not good enough)
- Self-sabotaging (I don't deserve succeed)
- Fear of success (Will my friends still like me?)
- Negative beliefs about success (Money is evil)
- Fear of failure (If I fail I will be humiliated)

The common denominator here is 'fear'. Fear is the leverage used by our established emotional set point to counteract our efforts to change.

Fear is the foundation of all our limiting beliefs.

> "Don't fear change, embrace it"
> -Anthony J. D'Angelo

To effectively overcome emotional homeostasis, we need to work at adopting empowering beliefs while simultaneously dismantling beliefs that limit us.

Chapter 6 - Modifying Your Beliefs is the longest and most involved chapter in this book. If you find yourself slipping into your old limiting beliefs at any point during this program, go back and review that information.

As you work your way through this information, pay close attention to any subtle influences that try to undermine your progress. When you become aware of a specific belief that is working against you, apply the dismantling techniques found in Chapter 6.

Every form of hidden fear that can affect your ability to change will eventually reveal itself. It will do so in the form of a disempowering belief. As soon as that happens, immediately use the skills you have learned to dismantle it.

When you destroy a limiting belief, amazingly the fear is destroyed along with it. In a later section, you will learn how to harness the energy that was once a fear, and then transform it into excitement and eager anticipation.

Section Review

We began this section by considering the power of having clearly defined goals.

Have you worked out the specifics of your goals?

Wants and desires are based on lack and scarcity. They focus on the problem rather than the solution.

Have you started to let go of this lacking mindset?

Intentions are much different than wants and desires. They move you to take action toward solutions.

Do you have an intended outcome for each of your goals?

Commitment is the key to results and trying invites failure because it is just wishful thinking.

Are you ready to commit to your own success?

Fear is the foundation of all limiting beliefs.

Are you on the lookout for limiting beliefs and ready to use the skills you've learned to dismantle them?

Section 4 - Path Connection

Designing Success

About Section 4

The path connection is where we tackle some of the practical building blocks involved in designing an actual success blueprint. This is where everything that you've done up to this point gets articulated into a workable outline.

You are about to finalize the details and put all your ducks in a row. You need to get ready to take action in a big way! By the time you finish this section, you will be fully prepared to explode into a highly focused pursuit of a meaningful goal.

This is the stage where you take an elusive dream and map it out so you can turn it into a reality. Success is never an accident. It follows a proven path that begins in your mind and heart, and moves purposely and predictably toward reality. You have the resources to create your dreams. Let's see how it looks on paper.

Chapters 14-17

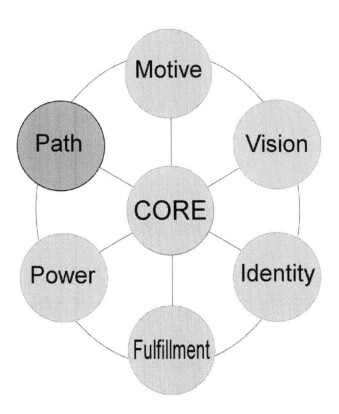

Chapter 14 -

Think It Through

We've all heard the quote, "Those who fail to plan, plan to fail." The question is - do you really believe that statement is true? Are you absolutely convinced of the value that comes from having a <u>well thought-out plan of action</u>?

Think about the difference between a spur of the moment, emotionally motivated decision, compared to a well thought-out and carefully planned one. In your experience, which scenario has a higher rate of success? When it comes to really important decisions in your life would you choose to rely on rational thinking or pure emotion?

The reason I chose the phrase "well thought-out plan of action" is because that is exactly what planning does; it causes us to think things through. It works like this. First you come up with a plausible course of action, and then you mentally follow it through to its logical conclusion. Along the way, you consider how things might work out for each of the steps needed to get from point A to point B.

Going through this thinking process a few times will result in a workable, step-by-step plan for reaching your goals. It's like having a map, with clearly defined mile markers to guide you along the way. You always know where you are going and why. You can also anticipate challenges that are likely to occur along the way.

I am not suggesting for a moment that life should be devoid of spontaneous decisions. Obviously, that wouldn't be any fun at all. Spontaneity certainly has its place, but when it comes to important areas of our life, you give yourself a big advantage by planning ahead and considering consequences.

> "Good plans shape good decisions.
> That's why good planning helps to make
> elusive dreams come true."
> -Lester Robert Bittel

When you intend to accomplish something, especially something extraordinary, your chance of success goes up astronomically when you follow a well thought-out plan of action. Planning is an important way to help ensure success.

One of the easiest ways to create a plan of action is to make a simple chart. I like to use a stair step format because the trend is always upward, constantly moving in the direction of my goal. This layout also reminds me of how each step (or short-term goal) contributes to the overall progression.

This is the same format that I used as a basis for this program, with each step building on the one that came before. Some steps cover more information than others, but the direction is always upward toward the goal.

For example, here's an overview of the seven sections of TRUE SELF laid out according to this format. The full size chart included a list of the chapters below each section, and key points below each chapter. This format allows for a lot of detail in a small space.

7 Connections

Core	Motive	Vision	Path	Power	Identity	Fulfillment
						Chapter Title
				Chapter Title	Chapter Title	
			Chapter Title	Chapter Title		
		Chapter Title	Chapter Title		- details	- details
	Chapter Title	Chapter Title	- details	- details	- details	- details
Chapter Title	Chapter Title	- details	- details	- details	- details	- details
- details	- details	- details	- details	- details	- details	- details

You can create a chart like this for any goal. Doing so will make it easier to identify each level of progress, while still allowing you to see the big picture.

The bigger your goal is, the more important it becomes to chart your progress. If you set a goal to lose 40 pounds within a certain time frame, having a progress chart would be more important than if you only need to lose 5 pounds. When you undertake a major goal, it is very easy to get so involved in any part of the process that you completely lose your sense of direction and timing.

Having a chart and a timetable provides momentum and prevents unnecessary detours. If this seems like too much trouble, then you should ask yourself how important your goal really is to you.

Any goal worth achieving is certainly worth the effort of creating an action plan. There is a huge difference between wishful thinking and effective goal planning. Success requires a well-articulated goal. It is not the product of wishful thinking.

Now, depending on your goal and what's at stake, coming up with a good plan may take a few minutes or a few weeks. You may be able to do it yourself or you might need to recruit some assistance. If you want to accomplish a goal outside of your personal expertise, do not hesitate to seek help in one form or another.

Trying to create a plan of action without all the facts can easily lead to disappointing results. Maybe you just need to do a little research to supplement your knowledge on the subject. By all means, do the research first before you create your plan of action.

Perhaps you need a teacher or coach to lay it out for you step-by-step. If so, then find someone qualified to help you.

Realize that time is your most valuable asset. Learning from those who have already invested their time and effort is the fastest way to get results. The purpose of your plan of action is so you will succeed in producing your intended result. By taking advantage of the knowledge that is already available, you can save time and avoid making costly mistakes.

"Planning is bringing the future into the present
so that you can do something about it now."
-Alan Lakein

Let's explore some additional ways to stay
on course while working on major goals.
For example, we can use…

Chapter 15 -

Mile Markers

Have you ever been traveling somewhere and found yourself on a very long stretch of unfamiliar highway with no road signs? You know you are traveling in the right direction, but you keep searching the roadside for reassurance.

How long can you keep driving before you begin to wonder, "Is this the right road? Did I miss the turn off?" Sooner or later, you will begin to doubt your direction. How long will it be before someone says, "Are we still on Hwy 78 or did we miss a turn somewhere?" If this goes on long enough you will start to think about turning around. "Maybe we should go back to that last turn off."

Then you see a sign up ahead, "Junction Hwy 95 - 7 miles ahead." All of a sudden everything is fine. Because of that one little sign you have been completely reassured. Yes, you are on course and you are even ahead of schedule. In 10 seconds you went from harboring feelings of doubt and uncertainty to being relaxed and confident.

On the roadway of personal development, we need signs and mile markers to avoid doubt and uncertainty. When we are traveling on an unfamiliar road, a line from point A to point B is simply not enough. We need a way to chart our progress in terms of distance covered and amount of time spent.

We need mile markers, the more the merrier! Let's revisit our example goal of wanting to lose 40 pounds from the last chapter. How would you chart this goal and what would you include? Obviously, you want to keep track of your weight loss in small, manageable increments. You also want to keep track of how fast you are actually losing the weight.

For the sake of this illustration, let's say you plan to lose 2 pounds per week. How does that pencil out? Two pounds per week times 20 weeks equals 40 pounds. Is this enough of a plan to successfully reach your goal?

How about calories? We need to know calories consumed compared to calories burned. Why? Because losing 2 pounds per week means we need to create a weekly calorie deficit of 7000 calories or 1000 calories per day. If we didn't have that information, what would happen to our chances of success?

Now we have a clear goal; lose 40 pounds in 20 weeks. Our goal is broken down into manageable steps that we can use as mile markers - lose 2 pounds per week. We also know that, through a combination of diet and exercise, we need to create a daily calorie deficit of 1000 calories.

Do we have enough information now to successfully reach our goal? Well, it's a start. We have enough to illustrate the value of mile markers and a timeline. But this is the point where you need to ask yourself, "How serious am I about losing those 40 pounds within the next 20 weeks?"

If you are totally committed to making that happen, then you're going to need more information. The greater your commitment to success, the more detailed and flexible your plan of action needs to be. Understanding what is involved helps ensure success.

If losing 40 pounds were easy, there would be a lot less overweight people. Charging into any important pursuit without a detailed plan based on an adequate number of facts is not the way to accomplish you goal.

Like most worthwhile goals, losing substantial amounts of body weight involves more than just a superficial knowledge and good intentions. Do you remember our discussion on homeostasis and set point? From here we could talk about macro and micronutrients, fat loss versus water weight or muscle loss, and so on. The point is, get the facts first!

All of this should serve to illustrate the incredible value of a well thought-out plan of action. Taking the time to carefully chart your course beforehand radically increases your chance for success. Knowing where you are going each step of the way eliminates doubt and builds confidence. Doing research or getting help lets you avoid costly mistakes and saves time.

There is another important benefit that makes your plan of action a worthwhile endeavor. It turns the whole process of setting and achieving goals into an enjoyable and rewarding experience. Proper planning actually makes it fun.

Isn't it true that we want to enjoy the entire process not just the results? In the bigger picture of personal development, each accomplished goal becomes another mile marker. We never stop growing and learning, so in reality, the value is in the journey. Living a truly rewarding life means enjoying all the different legs of your journey, each and every step.

Chapter 16 -

Date with Destiny

Having a set time to take action is a vital step on the path of success for many reasons. For starters, it creates anticipation and motivation. Think about a wedding. First the couple decides to get married. Next, they make wedding plans.

Then what do they do?

They set a precise date and time for the wedding to take place. What usually happens as that wedding date approaches? The energy level keeps climbing, arrangements are finalized and everyone involved works hard so the wedding can take place precisely on time.

Why? Because they set a precise time for that event, and their world rearranges itself to meet that deadline. It's absolutely amazing how much work can get done in a short period of time when people are trying to meet a deadline. Time frames help us to focus and to channel our energy so that we can accomplish our goals.

Businesses do this all the time, and it has a huge effect on the outcome of a product launch, movie release, or grand opening. They use the term "buzz" to describe the anticipation that precedes such an event. "Buzz" is the equivalent of positive energy. By establishing a precise time to begin taking action, you can harness megawatts of positive energy as well.

Having a precise time to begin taking focused action is one of the most important elements of a well thought-out goal strategy. It's what I like to call a <u>multiplier</u> because it allows you to harness a huge amount of energy and to multiply the effectiveness of all your efforts exponentially.

Once you have a clearly defined goal, a well thought-out plan of action and a precise time and date to launch into action, amazing things begin to happen. Your world begins to rearrange itself in a very focused way. As a result, energy in the form of anticipation begins to be generated at ever-increasing levels, as that date approaches.

In the world of goal realization, this particular stage of preparation could be likened to drawing back the line of an archer's bow. It takes effort to pull that line back and it takes focus to draw a bead on the bull's-eye.

But the archer's focus is on the target, not the process. His intended result is to see that arrow in the center of the target and that's where his attention is. In his mind it's already a done deal.

When you set a goal you need that same kind of focus and determination. In your mind, your goal needs to become a living, breathing thing. It needs to be so real to you that you can see it as if it's already accomplished. You can already feel the satisfaction of success. In your mind it needs to be a done deal. At that point, all that's left is for you to reach out and grab the prize.

This kind of mindset unlocks enormous resources that you may not even realize you have. Nobody knows the limits of human potential. What we do know is this: if you can see your goal clearly enough in your mind, then your mind believes that it already exists. When you tell your mind that something is real, you actually program it to help you create that reality.

> "You don't have to be great to get started,
> but you have to get started to be great."
> -Les Brown

There are always two sides to
every timetable. There's a time to
launch into action followed by a...

Chapter 17 -

Time for Completion

Depending on your project, this can be either the completion of one phase of a huge long-term effort, or a finish date for the entire project. Why is this so important?

Having a point of completion is like having a finish line in front of you. It gives you something specific to aim for. The closer you get to the finish line, the greater your focus and determination become. Focus and determination generate energy and create continued momentum.

The finish line represents success. It is the point of transition from reaching for your goal, to actually reaching your goal. Completion is where effort becomes accomplished. It's the point where you accept success in your life and acknowledge a job well done.

Reaching the finish line is a legitimate reason to celebrate and to feel really good about yourself. It's also a perfect opportunity to give yourself some well deserved approval.

As you move closer to the finish line, your anticipation of success can generate huge amounts of energy. This energy will allow you to blast through any obstacles that try to postpone or derail the completion of your project.

Without a clearly defined goal and a well thought-out plan of action, there is no way to know exactly where you are going. So how will you recognize it when you arrive? Knowing where you are going, and when you are supposed to get there is the only way to maintain your focus, and stay committed to your goal.

Successful accomplishment of a goal, any goal, is not about being the smartest guy on the block. It's not about luck, and it doesn't happen by accident. It's about following a proven, step-by-step process that will lead you where you want to go.

If you look around, you quickly realize that this is not some groundbreaking secret knowledge; this is simply how successful people get things done.

Here's a practical example. Let's say that you want to build a new house for your family. Just what does that process look like?

1. The first thing you need is a clearly defined goal; in this case, a new house.

2. Next, you need a well thought-out plan of action. You need to consider the needs of your family, your budget, the style and size of your new house, and the location. You also need someone to draw the blueprints.

3. Now you choose a contractor, and everyone agrees on when the project will start, how much it will cost, and when you can move in. Prior to beginning work on the house, your contractor will need to get permits, do some site work, and make sure the utilities are in place. Even though this preparation work is necessary for the project, it is not part of the actual house construction.

4. The day construction begins on the house there is a flurry of activity. Things begin to happen very quickly, and a huge amount of energy and excitement are generated. Very rapidly, you have a foundation, a floor, walls and then a roof. Every day brings you closer to your goal.

Notice that this does not happen haphazardly. There is a logical, systematic sequence that is followed according to the plan. Your contractor knows the process and he follows it. Why? Well, because he has committed his time, resources and crew to building your house. He has scheduled subcontractors and inspections ahead of time, and he is working hard to keep things running smoothly and on schedule. Why?

5. Because he's got a deadline to keep, and he's got another house to build after yours. Besides, that is when he gets paid and you get to move in. Everyone's reward and success is tied to the completion of this project, and the closer it gets to the finish line, the greater the anticipation.

In addition to building projects large and small, successful businesses, partnerships, and long-term personal relationships like marriage, all follow a similar process. Success in all these areas follows a proven process, in which each step is vital. All you have to do is follow the process, develop the skills, and you will accomplish amazing things.

"When we are motivated by goals that have deep meaning, by dreams that need completion, by pure love that needs expressing, then we truly live life"
-Greg Anderson

Section Review

An action outline has several important elements, and each one plays a key role in your success.

We discussed how a well thought out plan of action could dramatically increase your rate of success.

Do you have a plan of action for each of your goals?

We looked at an easy way to chart your action plan.

Is your chart broken down into progressive steps?

If your plan of action is well thought-out it includes:

1) *A workable timetable for each step*
2) *Mile markers so you can monitor progress*
3) *A specific date to launch into action*
4) *A set time for completion*

Time is the most valuable asset you have. Enlisting some experienced help can save you a lot of time.

Have you thought seriously about this option?

You are about to learn how to generate a tremendous amount of energy and focus it with laser precision.

Section 5 - Power Connection

Harness the Power

About Section 5

The Power Connection is all about launching into action and keeping the momentum going. This section includes all the elements of a highly focused adventure toward the successful completion of anything you want to accomplish.

There are proven methods for generating huge amounts of energy, and then turning that energy into enough momentum to move you quickly and decisively toward success. There are also some clever, and often overlooked, techniques to help you maintain laser sharp focus while continuing to take action.

Learning how to keep your eye on the ball is absolutely vital when you're playing to win. Distractions are everywhere and it's easy to lose your focus. Staying motivated and maintaining focus can be challenging. So let's see what it takes to overcome distractions and stay on course.

Chapters 18-23

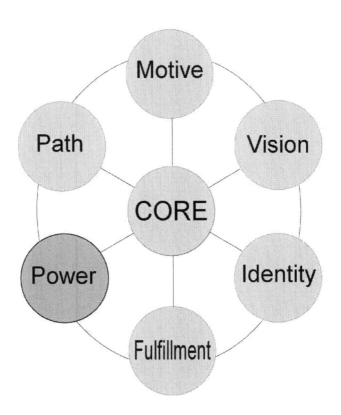

Chapter 18 -

The Power of Decision

What is it that can actually change the course of your life in a moment? In the quest for personal excellence what is the one, vital step we must take before we can take action? What is it that determines the actions that we take today, next week or next year?

Your future is shaped by the decisions you are making right now. The life you lead today is, to a very large degree, a result of the decisions you made in the past.

Many people think that conditions and circumstances are what determine the quality of their life. I agree that these things have an influence, and we may have to adjust our approach accordingly. But, in the long run, it's our ability to make wise decisions and to take appropriate action that will shape the quality of our life both now and in the future.

The most powerful decision we can make, in fact, the decision that we all must make, is to take total responsibility for everything that happens to us. That is the only way that you can put yourself in control of your own life.

"The controls for your life can only be reached
from the seat of responsibility."

As long as we hold the belief that our life is controlled
by outside forces, we will be tempted to make excuses
or pass the buck. Our self-sabotaging inner voice will
say; "there's nothing I can do about it" or "it's not my
fault, what can I do?"

The one sure way to eliminate such destructive self-
talk is to take full responsibility for everything. We
must make a decision to grab hold of the controls of
our own life and never hand them over to anyone else.
Put yourself permanently in the driver's seat.

We all face challenges, but do we view them as walls
or as hurdles? If it's a wall, make a decision to go
around it. If it's a hurdle, make a decision to jump over
it. It's not about what happens to you, or what gets in
front of you, it's what you decide to do about it.

One common reason why people's decisions don't
lead to the result they hoped for has to do with not
understanding what it really means to make a
decision. The term "decision" is so loosely applied

these days, that often what is being described is not a decision at all, but simply wishful thinking.

Preferences are not decisions. Saying something like "I'd like to", "I want to" or even "I'm planning to", is not a decision. These terms do not involve making any sort of commitment, and all true decisions involve commitment.

If there's no commitment, it's not a decision.

A commitment means that you are determined to stick with the decision you made and to achieve your intended result. No other option is acceptable.

Amazing things happen when our decisions go hand-in-hand with a total commitment. As a result, most people feel a tremendous amount of internal relief because now they have a clear objective.

Confusion tends to rob you of your power, whereas clarity will always empower you. Out of clarity and commitment comes decisive action.

It's important to realize that decision-making, like any other skill, improves with practice. The more often you make decisions, the more you'll come to realize that you truly are in control of your life. As a result, instead of challenges you will see opportunities. Instead of walls you will see hurdles that you now have the ability to leap over.

"Commitment gives muscle to your decisions."

Realize that being committed to following through on a decision does not mean being inflexible. As we begin to take action we will learn by experience how to make necessary adjustments to help bring about our intended result. This is part of the skill of decision-making and mastering it will elevate the quality of your life to the next level.

Understanding the power of our decisions to improve the quality of our life means that we must carefully consider the consequences of any decision we make. We do this before we commit to it, not after. This is one of the keys to gaining control over your life.

Rather than making decisions based on immediate gratification, it's vital that you consider the long-term results. Don't be fooled by the temptation of the quick fix.

It would be self-sabotaging to commit to any decision that is out of harmony with your personal values and standards. In addition, it is always counterproductive to choose any course of action that creates internal conflict.

Always examine your deeper motives and the possible internal consequences before making a commitment.

Decisions have the power to change your life in a moment only if they come with a total commitment to producing your intended result. If your decisions don't lead to action, then they really don't lead to anything except frustration.

There is a profound distinction between people who make the majority of their decisions consciously and those who merely go with the flow.

If you don't take control of your own decision-making process then you'll become a victim of circumstances. That too is a decision, it's the decision you make by trying to avoid the responsibility of making decisions. I like to say that there are three kinds of people in the world:

1) **Those who want something to happen**. These are generally people who don't understand the dynamics of decision-making and settle for wishful thinking.

2) **Those who make something happen**. These are the ones who make carefully considered decisions, a total commitment, and then take action.

3) **Those who wonder what happened**. These are people who avoid making decisions and then can't understand how they ended up where they are.

If you truly want to take control of your life, if you want to make something happen, it is absolutely vital that you develop your skills as a decision-maker.

Many people avoid making decisions because they're afraid of failing. For a skilled decision-maker, there is no such thing as failure, only results.

If we commit to a decision and follow through with action, we will produce results. If we don't produce the result we want, then we learn from the experience, make adjustments and continue.

Making a commitment means you are willing to persist until you produce your intended result. The only failure comes from giving up. If we give up because we didn't produce the results we wanted then the learning process stops.

Learning and adjusting is how we reach our goals. Every effort increases our knowledge base; the result is → we learn what works and what doesn't. This process also increases our skill level so we can make better decisions as we continue learning.

Are there areas in your life where you continually postpone making decisions? Have you given up on a goal because you didn't get the result you wanted the first time? Now would be a good time to put all that in the past. Why not make a fresh start today?

Often times the hardest step in achieving anything in your life is making the decision to do something about it now. Think about some area of your life that has been stalled because a decision needs to be made. Could you make that decision today, right now?

Start by re-examining the situation and give yourself three possible choices of action. Quickly think about the motives and consequences of each choice. Now pick the one that you think will produce the best, long-term result. Don't over analyze the situation; in your heart you know which choice is the right one, make it.

Now make a total commitment to follow through on your decision. Start by taking immediate action. Continue taking action and making adjustments until you achieve your intended result. You don't need to know every detail of your action plan before you begin. Taking action helps you find solutions, so go ahead and get started today.

Congratulations, you have just taken one of the most important steps toward gaining control of your life. If you stay the course, your life will never be the same. The more often you make decisions and follow through on them, the more skilled you will become.

> Decision-making can involve a certain degree of fear. What if the <u>fear</u> energy could be reframed?

Chapter 19 -

Fear, Anticipation & Excitement

Fear is like a two-sided coin. If we control it, we can use it to our benefit. On the flipside, if fear controls us, it will render us unable to accomplish anything.

Think about a roller coaster ride. Part of what moves people to get on a roller coaster is the fear, except they don't call it fear, do they? No, they call it *excitement*.

What makes it possible to embrace a fearful situation and see it as exciting and exhilarating? In the case of a roller coaster, you see others doing it and having fun. No one flew out of their seat, and all the cars stayed on the track. So your mind becomes convinced that you won't die.

This is where the negotiation process begins between your mind (logic) and your emotions (fear). Your mind says, "You can do this and it will be fun." How these internal negotiations turn out will have a lot to do with your level of fear and the reasons behind that fear. These are your paradigms.

Suppose that as a child, you saw someone fall to their death from a roller coaster. Obviously, in that case, your fear is deeply ingrained and your mind will probably never be able to move past it, period. In fact, your mind will likely support your emotions and your inner dialogue will be short and unchangeable. "I'm not getting on that thing no matter what."

There is nothing wrong with that kind of reaction. It is a natural, survival response that serves to protect you from danger. That is why sane people don't try to jump off of tall buildings in hopes of flying. So fear can be a healthy, logical response to a dangerous situation, and that's a good thing.

Now, let's go back to the internal negotiations about the roller coaster ride. For someone with no fearful roller coaster references, what's the likely outcome? Their mind will be able to reframe the fearful energy into anticipation of an exciting experience.

In this situation, the person whose mind is energized by a manageable amount of fear will be able to create a positive internal response, which opens the door to a positive and exciting experience.

Because the human mind is capable of processing billions of bits of information per second, all of this can take place in a moment. So, most of the time, we just respond on autopilot without considering what's involved.

This is where things get interesting. Let's say we made a decision to get on that roller coaster and have some fun. So far, everything that has happened has been internal. We haven't really done anything yet, except make a choice. That choice must be turned into action before we can experience any results.

Now we come to the *decisive moment*. The special moment in time when we commit to following through by taking action on the decision we've made.

With reference to our roller coaster ride, it becomes a commitment at the *decisive moment* when we climb aboard, place the safety bar across our lap and the cars start to move. Now we can get excited. Now our whole being becomes focused on this "experience" because we have made a commitment and we can't go back.

For someone who has never been on a roller coaster ride before, the actual experience will probably be far more intense than they had imagined.

When we experience something firsthand, we often find that much more is involved than we were expecting. The level of sensory stimulation may require us to hold on tighter and tighter while our adrenaline levels rise and our body rushes from a negative G force to a positive one.

Without a decisive moment and total commitment, we will never know the rush of excitement or the sense of satisfaction that comes from reframing our fears.

> That means that the launch pad for accomplishing your intended result is...

Chapter 20 -

The Decisive Moment

For an Olympic track athlete, the **decisive moment** comes when he brings to the starting line the sum total of all his training and focus, assumes the starting posture, the gun fires and he rockets into action.

At that moment his energy levels explode, his focus is unshakable and his commitment is absolute. You can use this same concept to propel you into truly focused action.

The decisive moment occurs when planning and preparation are transformed into action driven by a total commitment to success. The surest way to accomplish incredible things in your life is to bring that same level of commitment and focus to the starting line before you launch into action.

Setting a goal, establishing a plan of action and fixing on a specific time to start, are all vital to success, but they actually make up the training and preparation phase. These are the steps that prepare you for the action phase.

Yes, each step required you to make choices and then act on those choices. Each step also moved you closer to your goal. But everything changes at the **decisive moment**. From that point on it is a new and completely different experience. It's game time.

This is the moment when you blow the doors off your limitations and you call up resources you didn't even realize you had. At this point, any residual fear becomes excitement, doubt vanishes and your commitment gives you the focus needed to blast through anything that tries to get in your way.

Now it's a rush, a living roller coaster ride and you are the one having fun.

> But to fully harness that incredible energy you absolutely must make a...

Chapter 21 -

Total Commitment

A total commitment is absolutely vital! **The level of your commitment will be reflected in the level of your success**. Commitment is like rocket fuel when it comes to reaching your goals, especially the big ones.

Total commitment is what allows otherwise ordinary people to accomplish extraordinary success. This basic rule applies to every area of human endeavor. Let's look at a common example.

When two people exchange marriage vows they promise to stay together, no matter what, and to love and honor each other through thick and thin.

Obviously, some take those promises more seriously than others because in the United States more than 50% of all marriages fail. What is the primary underlying cause?

Some people are much more committed to having a successful marriage than others are. At one point or another, married life will test your level of commitment.

A successful marriage, like any other worthwhile goal, requires a total commitment. And, just like any other worthwhile goal, the reward for success can be far greater than we ever imagined. But without a real commitment to success we will never know.

Remember our example of the roller coaster ride? Once that thing started moving we were committed because there was no way out except to see it through to the end. We were locked in for the duration. Some might feel this is restrictive.

In reality, it's the security of being locked in that makes it possible to turn fear into excitement.

Once you let go of all the "what ifs" and accept the fact that you are in something for the duration, amazing and unexpected things will begin to happen. This is when your untapped resources become available. You have unlocked them with your total commitment.

One of the reasons this happens is that now you are required to focus on success instead of escape. It becomes necessary to find ways of overcoming challenges rather than running away from them. As you tap into your hidden resources, you will be amazed by your own insights and abilities.

But here's something that very few people realize. Once you have harnessed the power of a decisive moment and propelled yourself forward with a total commitment, your world will begin to rearrange itself to support you.

By now, everyone is aware of the Law of attraction and millions of people have watched "The Secret." In reality though, very few people have been able to make the Law of attraction work in their own behalf.

Here's the reason why: Lots of folks have the belief that once they have a clearly defined goal, they can just sit around and focus on it, and somehow it will manifest in their life. Sorry, that is not how it works.

Notice I didn't say, "It doesn't work." I said, "That is not how it works." When you think about the Law of attraction, think in terms of action and reaction.

When you move from thinking about a goal to a well-thought-out plan, you are taking action. When you set a starting date and prepare to meet it, you are taking action.

But when your decisive moment comes, and you move from planning mode to full action mode with a total commitment, everything changes.

Now, the Law of Attraction (what I like to call the quantum feedback loop) is at your service.

If you watched the movie 'The Secret,' you will have noticed that the people interviewed in that movie are perfect examples of this. Consider Joe Vitale, this guy is a man of action.

The number of books this man has written is amazing. Does he believe in the Law of attraction? Absolutely! He knows from firsthand experience that it works. In fact, it is a major force behind his success.

Does he sit around thinking about success until it drops in his lap?

No! He makes a total commitment to writing and promoting each new book. The Law of attraction can now respond to his level of action and commitment and his personal willingness to accept success.

This is a perfect example of a quantum feedback loop. Let's examine the two major forces involved so you can be absolutely clear about what's required.

1) <u>You must be willing to allow yourself to accept success into your life.</u> This is one of the reasons we spent so much time in Section 1 learning how to clear away limiting beliefs. You must believe that you deserve it.

2) <u>You need commitment and action to activate the energy loop connected to your intended outcome.</u> It's how we open up the gate and step into the energy flow.

What you are able to attract will depend entirely on your willingness to accept it and the amount of energy you focus toward it.

You must take action in harmony with your goals. As you continue to act, your own potential will expand. You will become a magnet, attracting whatever you need to keep taking action as your path continues to unfold before you.

When you make a total commitment to success there is only one direction you can move - forward. The reason most people never have this experience is not because they can't do it. Rather, it is because they don't understand what it takes to get massive momentum started.

"Life's rewards go to those who let
their actions rise above their excuses."
-Lee J. Colan

Chapter 22 -

A Question of Focus

One of the major differences between people and their outlook on life is the questions that they consistently ask themselves.

Questions have the ability to change our focus in an instant. Asking the right questions can change your mindset from a limiting one to an empowering one. Your personal view of reality hinges on what your mind is focused on. Questions are one of the fastest and simplest ways to completely change your mental focus.

We are all in the habit of asking ourselves questions every day, but most of the time we are not even aware of their effect. Our minds love it when we ask ourselves questions.

Questions provide the mind with incentive and direction. As soon as we ask a question, our mind immediately begins searching for an answer. If we don't like the answers we are getting, it's probably because we are not asking the right questions.

"The fastest way to change the answers
you receive from yourself and others is to
change the questions you ask." -Lee J. Colan

Questions have a dramatic effect on everything we do in life. They determine our abilities, the quality of our relationships and our income. By consistently asking the right questions we can empower ourselves to change any aspect of our life.

So, just what are the right questions and how do they shape our lives?

Questions that cause us to focus on possibilities and solutions are the ones that empower us.

The problem is that we can easily slip into the habit of asking ourselves questions that are limiting, or even mentally and emotionally disabling.

Whatever we focus on the most, will eventually become our reality. By consciously training ourselves to consciously ask empowering questions, regardless of our circumstances, we will direct our minds to continually focus on new possibilities and solutions. This is exactly the kind of focus that enhances our personal growth and development.

Now let's look at a couple of situations that could arise and notice how asking different types of questions can radically alter our mental disposition.

Say it's Wednesday morning and the alarm just went off. What's the first question you ask yourself? If you say, "Why do I have to go to work today?" how is that going to affect your attitude? If you say "Why do I feel so tired and run down?" how is that going to affect your energy levels?

With those two simple questions, you have set yourself up for a disappointing day. Why? Because now your mind is focused on finding reasons why you're tired, and why you have to do something you apparently don't want to do.

What if the first two questions you asked yourself were, "What do I have to look forward to today?" and "What am I most grateful for right now?" Even if you don't have the immediate answers to those questions, your mind will focus on finding the answers. Ask yourself those questions a few times and notice how the answers make you feel. All of a sudden you have something to look forward to and something to be grateful for. How will that kind of mindset affect your day?

Here's another situation. Suppose someone makes a thoughtless comment to you, what's the first question you ask yourself? If you ask, "Why don't they like me?" how will that make you feel? Probably pretty bad, because now your mind is looking for reasons why people don't like you and the answers are not going to be very encouraging.

But what if your response was, "I wonder what I can do to help them feel better?" As your mind searches for the answer to that question, you are going to be focused in a positive direction. That's because you will be busy searching for a way to help someone else.

As we can plainly see, asking the right questions of ourselves can produce very positive results. The real challenge here is that we tend to operate on automatic pilot. Most of the time we fail to take conscious control of the questions we are repeatedly asking ourselves. Consequently, growing your awareness of what is involved will help you develop this ability.

As human beings, we can only focus on a limited number of things at any given time. We can use this trait to our advantage, because when we focus on empowering things it is pretty much impossible to focus on limiting thoughts at the same time.

Can you be truly happy and extremely sad at the same time? Can you feel intense love and intense anger simultaneously? Possibly, but only in extremely rare situations.

Normally, we cannot intensely focus our attention in two opposing directions at the same time. This means that when we focus on something positive, really focus on it, our minds will push aside or block out negative thoughts.

Because questions have the ability to change our focus, we can automatically change our feelings at the same time. When you ask yourself, "What do I feel really great about right now?" your mind becomes occupied with answering that question; it simply cannot search for reasons to feel good and feel lousy at the same time.

Some people are convinced that they can entertain opposing thoughts simultaneously. At the very least, doing that requires a mental and emotional compromise. It requires that we apply only limited focus in two different directions. Some synonyms for the verb focus are: concentrate, fixate and pinpoint. Once we understand what focus really means, we realize that it does not allow for divided attention.

Being truly focused involves more than just our mental acuity; it also requires our emotional involvement. This is especially true because the questions we are asking ourselves have to do with the way we feel. When we ask those questions we are commanding our mind to give us answers that will support the way we prefer to feel.

Emotions are the power plant of human motivation. We can use our minds to ask the right questions to harness that power, and focus it in the direction we want to go.

Let's look at a few examples of questions that will help us accomplish this.

When problems arise in life, as they will, what questions can we ask ourselves to move us toward possibility and solution?

1) How does this problem or challenge create a new opportunity? At first, you may not see opportunity, so keep asking. This question is powerful because it is structured around the assumption that the problem has created an opportunity, now you just need to

discover what it is. Your mind will recognize that assumption and before long will present you with a list of possible opportunities.

2) What action must I take to transform this situation? Notice the assumption built into this question. There is a course of action that will transform the situation; all you need to do is find it.

3) What aspect of this challenge is exciting? Again the assumption, there's something here to get excited about. We just asked our mind to figure out what that is, and it will figure it out.

Did you notice what all of these questions have in common?

They all have a built-in assumption that moves our focus in a positive direction. They all create a frame of reference that is empowering. And because we can focus in only one direction at a time, all of these questions prevent us from exploring the negative aspects of our situation, both mentally and emotionally.

Applying these three questions in challenging situations will require a conscious effort at first. It takes time to develop a pattern of asking empowering questions, especially when our resources are challenged by problems. With practice, however, we can condition ourselves to respond resourcefully to any situation.

Okay, now that you have begun to build an appreciation for the value of using questions to change both your focus and mindset, there are a couple of things that need to be considered.

The first point we want to examine is - How can we develop the pattern of intentionally using questions to direct our focus and control our mindset?

As with anything else, when we want to develop a pattern, we need to practice that activity. That means we need to practice intentionally using questions that direct our minds and emotions in a constructive way.

Try this experiment: Every morning when you wake up, it's a natural part of your thinking process to ask yourself questions about the upcoming day, so this is a perfect opportunity to practice. Asking the right questions first thing in the morning will help ensure that your focus is pointed in a productive and empowering direction.

Here's a list of possible questions that you can begin asking yourself every morning starting first thing tomorrow morning. These questions are designed to have an effect on your levels of joy, commitment and self-esteem.

1) What is it about my life that makes me feel happy right now?
2) What is going on in my life today that I can get excited about?
3) What do I feel truly grateful for right now?
4) What am I really looking forward to today?
5) Whom do I love and who loves me?

If you have difficulty answering any of these questions simply insert the word "could" into the question. For example, in question #1- What is it about my life that could make me feel happy right now?

Take some time to consider these questions as you go about your morning routine. Keep in mind that the questions determine the direction of your thoughts, but it's the answers that create the desired result. So, as you answer each question, take a moment to fully experience how that answer makes you feel.

By developing a routine of asking yourself questions like these in the morning, you will begin to create a pattern. After a while, not only will the questions come automatically, but so will your level of appreciation for the answers. The answers to these questions make an important contribution to a life that is truly worth living.

Being aware of our blessings first thing in the morning can completely change the way we view our entire day. Those questions will accompany you throughout the day as you find yourself looking for more reasons to feel happy, to get excited, and to feel grateful.

This is an example of the power of simple questions to change the focus, motivation and results we experience in every aspect of life. Remember, the whole purpose of this exercise is to take conscious control of what we allow our minds to focus on.

A second important point to consider is this; these questions are designed to trigger our minds into thinking in a positive direction and to lead us to discover encouraging answers. They are not designed to over-analyze or scrutinize our every thought and feeling. Don't let yourself get too carried away. Know when to quit asking and start enjoying the answers.

When you design questions for yourself, make sure that they include a positive assumption about the answer. All of the example questions are built around an assumption.

Question one assumes that there is something to feel happy about right now just as question two assumes there is something to be excited about.

These type of assumptions give your mind both direction and motivation. Constructing your own personal questions this way will empower you with the ability to change your life.

"We make our world significant by the courage
of our questions and by the depth of our answers."
-Carl Sagan

Closely related to the questions we ask is the language we use. There's power in words.

Chapter 23 -

The Power of Words

We all recognize that we get results by taking action - no action, no results! We are also aware that there are a variety of motivators that can move us to take action. One of the greatest challenges in personal development is learning to control those motivators so that we intentionally move ourselves to take action and produce results at will.

Emotions are the most powerful of all the forces that move us to take action in our lives. Developing the ability to use our minds to harness and direct our emotional power is one of the best ways to insure that we consistently produce our intended results.

This is where words come into play. Not just any words, but a special group of words I will refer to as our emotional vocabulary. For the sake of this discussion, let's imagine that we are going to divide all of the words we know into two different groups.

We will call the first and largest group, our functional vocabulary. These are the words we use regularly to communicate thoughts and ideas with no particular emotional value. The second group, although smaller than the first, is much more powerful. This is what I call our emotional vocabulary. These are the words that we use to communicate our feelings, not just to the outside world, but also to ourselves.

Our emotional vocabulary is made up of word labels that we assign to our various feelings. We have word labels for intense feelings, both positive and negative, just as we have word labels for less intense feelings that are either positive or negative. How is this information useful?

Because we use word labels to describe how we feel about the different experiences in our life, changing the label can actually alter the way we interpret the experience.

For example, if we have a wonderful experience that leaves us feeling absolutely overjoyed, but represent that experience by saying, "that was nice," then we minimize the intensity and the joy associated with that experience. This also works the other way around. If we have an experience that is only "pleasant" but we label it as "absolutely wonderful," it will change our feelings about that experience.

We will have fortified the experience with a greater degree of positive emotional intensity simply by changing the word label we used to represent it.

Consider the implications:

By giving conscious attention to the word labels that we habitually use to represent our feelings, we can amplify the intensity of our positive experiences, and we can minimize the intensity and feelings associated with our negative experiences.

Without being aware of it, many people unintentionally magnify the negative experiences in their life, and at the same time, minimize their positive experiences. Using our emotional vocabulary in this way is a proven recipe for creating an ongoing, unpleasant, negative life experience.

We all have positive and negative experiences in life. Our view of those experiences and the impact they have on us will be determined by the way we interpret those experiences. Here's the bottom line, we can control the value and intensity of any experience by choosing word labels that represent those experiences in a way that empowers us.

We know that the mind works in pictures, not words. That being the case, how can words radically alter our feelings if the mind files everything as a picture?

It is true that we can picture something in our minds without having words to describe it. But, once you have a picture in your mind that you want to communicate to someone, what's the first thing you do? Isn't it true that you try to find the right words to describe that picture? It's a labeling process that facilitates our desire to communicate.

Even though our mental file cabinets are filled with pictures that represent experiences, we use words to access those files. The word labels that we use for those experiences tell our nervous system where they are filed. So the word labels, in effect, come to represent the whole experience, not just a description of the experience.

Before you can articulate a feeling or experience, you need words to describe it. If the words you use are not accurate you will misrepresent that experience to others. Now here's the fascinating thing about that, you will also misrepresent that experience to yourself. Why not use this fact to your advantage?

One of our personal goals should be to try and remain in the most resourceful mental state possible, even under adverse circumstances. When we are in a negative headspace, it tends to rob us of our resourcefulness.

Alternately, a positive headspace always increases our resourcefulness. The more resourceful we feel, the more motivated we are to take action. When we lack resources, we also lack motivation.

This is where we can use words to motivate ourselves to take action. We shift our perception by using word labels to describe our experiences in ways that are empowering.

How resourceful do you feel when you're infuriated? Think about that for a minute. Imagine yourself totally infuriated, and note how you feel. Now notice what happens to those feelings if you change the label from infuriated to mildly annoyed. Not only will you feel less angry, but you also feel more resourceful.

Let's take it one step farther. What if you represent that experience by saying to yourself, "I was mildly annoyed but it passed quickly." How does that affect your degree of resourcefulness?

Can you see the practical application of this information? Feeling resourceful equates to feeling motivated, and feeling motivated leads to taking action. The more ways we find to stay in a resourceful mental state, the more likely we will be to keep taking positive action in the direction of our goals and aspirations.

It's a clinical fact that more and more people are suffering from depression these days. Depression is a debilitating state of mind that leaves people feeling helpless and hopeless. This is the polar opposite of feeling empowered and motivated.

In his book *Awaken the Giant Within*, author Anthony Robbins describes one man's long standing battle against depression.

After explaining to the man the effect his words were having on his emotional state, the man agreed to the following. For the next 10 days he promised not to use the word 'depressed,' not even once. If he felt tempted to use that word he would replace it by saying, "I'm feeling a little bit down, I'm getting better, or I'm turning things around."

Simply shifting the word label used to describe his feelings completely changed his pattern of thinking. The level of pain that he experienced decreased which helped him stay in a more resourceful mental state.

Two years later that man said that he had not felt depressed, not even once, since he agreed to stop using the word 'depressed' to describe his feelings. By changing the word label, he totally changed his experience.

> "Words, when well chosen, have so great a force in them, that a description often gives us more lively ideas than the sight of things themselves."
> -Joseph Addison

Now imagine the effect on your life if you consistently and purposely diminished the emotional impact of your negative experiences, and simultaneously intensified your positive experience.

Life is full of challenges. Staying motivated in the face of such challenges will have a dramatic effect on the quality of your life. Will we learn from our challenges, or be devastated by them? Much will depend on our resourcefulness at the time. Learning to represent our experiences in empowering ways is a huge step in the right direction.

Section Review

Mastering the art of decision-making has the power to completely transform your life.

Did you finally make a decision you'd been avoiding?

We learned that it is possible to reframe fear and turn that energy into anticipation and excitement.

Have you considered doing this with any personal fears that might be holding you back from taking action?

Pinpointing the decisive moment when your planning turns to action can create massive momentum.

Have you isolated the decisive moment for your goal?

Many people avoid a total commitment and then they wonder why they don't produce their intended result.

Are you convinced that a total commitment has power?

Asking the right questions of ourselves will completely change our focus and our attitude.

Have you started asking yourself questions that allow you to focus on possibilities and solutions?

Do your questions include a built in assumption that has an empowering effect on you emotionally?

Our emotional vocabulary can control the value and the intensity of our experiences in life.

Have you been changing the word labels you use to describe your experiences in a way that empowers you?

Section 6 - Identity Connection

Accept Success

About Section 6

We all want success. However, if we are not prepared to accept success on an emotional level, bad things can happen. Success has a way of exposing hidden self-destruct tendencies that can turn our greatest accomplishments into liabilities.

The Identity connection is designed to assure that we are not only comfortable with our successes, but also satisfied with them. We spent considerable time identifying our real self in the early chapters. You already know that your identity as a successful person does not hinge on the results you produce. That knowledge creates a perfect foundation for allowing success to flow into your life.

The next few chapters will give you specific ways to make sure that success feels really rewarding and meaningful. You will learn how to anchor each of your new accomplishments in a way that satisfies your core desire for self-approval.

Chapters 24-27

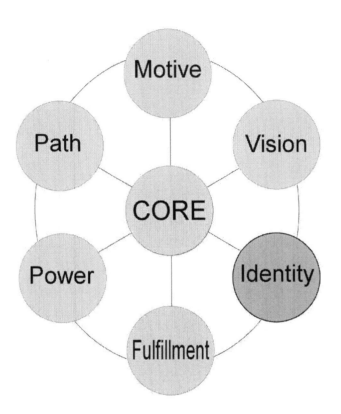

Chapter 24 -

Can You Handle It?

Following the steps outlined in this program so far has brought you face to face with success. Not just in one area, but in your whole life. Beginning with step one; you have learned powerful skills to untangle and rearrange yourself on the deepest levels.

Discovering your personal values and passions has allowed you to weave them into the fabric of your emotional identity. You have learned how to amplify all that is good and pleasurable in your life and dismantle or reframe what is not.

Let's face it, if you have applied what you've learned, and completed the exercises - then you are not the same person you were when you began this program. The fact is you have re-created yourself from the inside out, from your core.

What is the result? You have started to discover, and will continue to discover your true self. And it is very likely that your world is beginning to respond accordingly. By changing who you are, you have changed how you experience your life. You are well on your way to becoming the architect of your own reality.

You have allowed yourself to become a magnet for success on every level, both internally and externally. This will dramatically affect how others view you. It will also change the kind of opportunities that open up to you. As long as you continue to develop the skills you have acquired, your life will continue to expand in the direction of your choosing.

The question is - can you handle that?

I know it sounds like a crazy question. But rest assured I did not intend it as sarcasm. This is a question that needs to be asked. Are you emotionally prepared to accept success into every area of life? Are you willing to allow yourself to fully embrace the identity of an exceptionally happy and successful person?

Success has a strange effect on some people. There are countless, true stories about people who allowed success to become their downfall. If you think about it for a minute, you can probably name several, especially in the entertainment industry.

If you are reasoning that this only applies to those who succeed on a massive scale, think again.

Any degree of success in any area of life can trigger a hidden, self-destruct, response pattern. This happens when somewhere, deep down, you feel that you are undeserving.

Ironic, isn't it? People search for years to find that special someone to share their life with. Then for some reason, usually one that they are completely unaware of, they sabotage the relationship. Determined entrepreneurs struggle for years to build a successful business and then stop doing the very things that created their success.

Why do things like this happen? Because achieving success in one area will always expose insecurities in another. It becomes an internal struggle on the battlefield of pain and pleasure. This is one of the reasons why section one of this program is so important. Internal harmony will allow you to embrace your successes and to cultivate them.

If there is internal conflict, it will always surface in the environment of success.

If for any reason you skimmed through step one, then you have put yourself at risk. If that is the case, please go back and do the exercises. Remember, this is an investment you are making in yourself, and in your future. Being true to your personal code of ethics creates internal harmony. Pursuing your ethical passions adds a strong sense of joy and enthusiasm to your life. Constructively modifying your beliefs builds confidence and turns fear into excitement.

Reading about these things will encourage you, but only by doing them will you be fully prepared for success. A person who is internally successful can easily accept and savor all the successes they have created. Make up your mind to be that person. Get comfortable with your new identity. Embrace success.

> Deep down, what is it we all crave? Isn't it...

Chapter 25 -

Acknowledgment & Approval

At this point I want you to become completely aware of your accomplishments. When we are all wrapped up in doing, we tend to focus on each specific task. To fully appreciate the scope of our accomplishments, it is a good idea to step back and look at the big picture.

Taking some time to personally reflect on all the progress you have made will give you a whole new perspective.

When you walk through a forest you can only focus on one tree at a time. When you relocate to a scenic viewpoint, you can take in the whole panorama.

It is absolutely vital that you stop and acknowledge all that you have accomplished and give yourself approval. This is important because of the three core desires that are common to all people. They are:

1) The desire for approval
2) The desire for control
3) The desire for security

Most people are seeking ways to fulfill these desires from outside themselves. They want the approval of others. They want to control situations. And they look to money or friends for a sense of security. They are looking in all the wrong places.

> "It may be called the Master Passion,
> the hunger for self-approval." -Mark Twain

Yes, we all want approval, control, and security. Perhaps without your ever being aware of it, this program has already helped you fulfill those desires from within yourself. That is the way it should be, and must be, for a person with a successful, emotional identity.

Let's take a few minutes to review some of your accomplishments and notice how they provide an internal source of fulfillment for each of these basic desires.

The Desire for Approval

Chapters 1 and 2 helped you to see the need for upgrading your personal values to support your sense of internal harmony. What a great basis for approving of yourself, deciding to live according to what you know to be right and ethical.

You also formulated some guiding principles to assure yourself of continued approval. Adhering to these principles will serve to protect you from creating reasons to disapprove of yourself.

Chapter 3 further supported your efforts by teaching you to associate pleasure with doing good, and pain with doing bad, according to your personal code of ethics.

Chapters 4-6 taught you a number of skills to help align your passions, response patterns, and beliefs with the core values that you had already approved.

In essence, the chapters of section one gave you a sound and realistic basis for approving of yourself. By continuing to act in harmony with your true self, you will always have legitimate reasons to give yourself approval.

Looking to others for approval and validation usually indicates that we haven't given approval to ourselves.

"The most splendid achievement of all is
the constant striving to surpass yourself and
to be worthy of your own approval" -Denis Waitley

Some people feel that to accomplish their goals requires compromising their principles. You now know that this is false reasoning that can only lead to internal conflict.

Standing by your guiding principles has elevated the quality of your life to a higher standard. Think about that. What an incredible accomplishment. If you'll just stop and consider that for a moment, I believe you'll want to acknowledge this incredible accomplishment, and to give yourself the approval that you truly deserve. Why not take the time to do that right now? Allow yourself to bask in the warmth of your own approval.

Next up - the Desire for Control

Why do people feel a need for control? The fact that so much in their life is seemingly beyond their control is a major contributor. If we focus on what we cannot control, we begin to believe that gaining control is the solution to our problems. It's not!

The real problem here is the misguided concept that external influences determine who we are as a person. Yes, we all take cues from our surroundings. It is true that much of our time is spent adjusting our course of action to navigate through the changing circumstances of our day. But that is not who we are as a person.

Let's face it; you cannot control the weather, traffic, neighbors, workmates or world events. The question that begs an answer is this: will they control you? If you allow that to happen, you will never be able to fill your desire for control. Instead of feeling in control, you will feel like a victim of your circumstances.

You are not your circumstances and you are not a product of your environment. Everything in this program is designed to help you see that you are the architect of your own reality. It's not about what goes on around you; it's what you make of it.

You are in control. Learn to accept that.

In control of what? For starters, your TRUE SELF is in control of your values, passions and beliefs. That means that you are free to assign any value that you choose to the things going on around you.

You will never control all of the people and events you are exposed to. But you can always control your own beliefs about what those things mean. You decide how much something does or does not matter.

So while you may not literally control those external things, you do control how they affect you as a person. What does that mean to you right now?

For all intents and purposes, you are in complete control of your reality. You get to decide what your perception of any person, place or thing is, and what value that has in your life.

Have you accepted that control? There is no reason for you to desire control because you already have it. All you need to do is to accept it.

Chapters 7-17 taught you several effective ways to exercise control over the results you produce in your life. You learned how to take your successful mindset and systematically apply it to produce your intended outcome.

Control is power. In section five you learned how to harness that power. Chapters 18-21 showed you how to generate huge amounts of energy and direct that energy with laser sharp focus.

Chapters 22 and 23 gave you some very powerful techniques to stay motivated and on course as you worked toward the accomplishment of your goals.

If that isn't control, then what is?

Do you fully appreciate the scope of what you have already accomplished? In a world that is spinning out of control, you have managed to claim control over your life.

As you continue to exercise that control, don't be surprised at the powerful influence you will begin to have on the people and events around you. No doubt you will come to be recognized as a stabilizing influence and your environment will naturally respond accordingly.

Remember, control is power so make sure you stay true to your values and beliefs.

The Desire for Security

This is the granddaddy of all human emotions. Every person on the planet has an inherent and insatiable desire to feel safe and secure. Efforts to fill this desire shape the actions of individuals and the course of world events.

Just as the Earth is in orbit around the sun, human behavior revolves around the need for a physical and emotional sense of security.

Every inappropriate emotion that is not due to a chemical imbalance is due to feelings of insecurity. From the ancient civilizations to the new millennium, human history is a reflection of mankind's inability to fill this desire.

Wanting to feel safe and secure is closely tied to our survival instinct. This explains its position above all other emotions.

The chart on the next page represents some of the unproductive emotions that stem from and contribute to a sense of insecurity. It is by no means complete, but it makes a good reference.

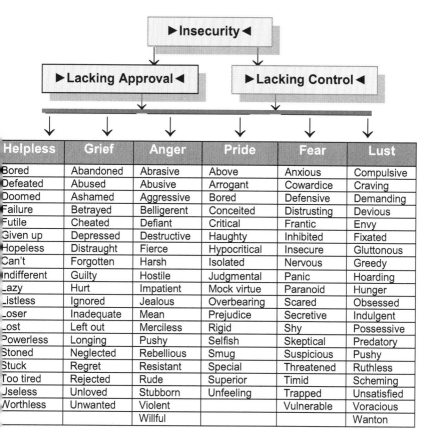

Helpless	Grief	Anger	Pride	Fear	Lust
Bored	Abandoned	Abrasive	Above	Anxious	Compulsive
Defeated	Abused	Abusive	Arrogant	Cowardice	Craving
Doomed	Ashamed	Aggressive	Bored	Defensive	Demanding
Failure	Betrayed	Belligerent	Conceited	Distrusting	Devious
Futile	Cheated	Defiant	Critical	Frantic	Envy
Given up	Depressed	Destructive	Haughty	Inhibited	Fixated
Hopeless	Distraught	Fierce	Hypocritical	Insecure	Gluttonous
Can't	Forgotten	Harsh	Isolated	Nervous	Greedy
Indifferent	Guilty	Hostile	Judgmental	Panic	Hoarding
Lazy	Hurt	Impatient	Mock virtue	Paranoid	Hunger
Listless	Ignored	Jealous	Overbearing	Scared	Obsessed
Loser	Inadequate	Mean	Prejudice	Secretive	Indulgent
Lost	Left out	Merciless	Rigid	Shy	Possessive
Powerless	Longing	Pushy	Selfish	Skeptical	Predatory
Stoned	Neglected	Rebellious	Smug	Suspicious	Pushy
Stuck	Regret	Resistant	Special	Threatened	Ruthless
Too tired	Rejected	Rude	Superior	Timid	Scheming
Useless	Unloved	Stubborn	Unfeeling	Trapped	Unsatisfied
Worthless	Unwanted	Violent		Vulnerable	Voracious
		Willful			Wanton

Be aware, these emotions are counterproductive; use
this chart as a reference to help you avoid them.
If we allow ourselves to indulge in these feelings they
will create in us an overall sense of insecurity that can
quickly undermine our progress.

This does not mean that we will never have these feelings, because we will. But remember, being in control gives you the power to dismantle any thought pattern or belief that does not support your personal growth.

There is an old saying, "you can't stop a bird from landing on your head, but you don't have to let it build a nest there." The point is; we all have inappropriate thoughts from time to time. What we decide to do with those thoughts is what really matters.

Will we focus on them, allowing them to grow? Or will we recognize them for what they are and discard them immediately? We always have a choice.

<u>Never allow yourself to entertain these feelings for any length of time. They are poison!</u>

The best way to feel secure is to continue to strengthen your internal feelings of approval and control. Just as insecurity is supported by a lack of approval and a lack of control, your sense of security is supported by feelings of approval and control.

Internal harmony is one of the best ways to protect yourself from feelings of insecurity. Knowing who you are, what you stand for, and where you are going is a strong foundation for feeling secure. Acting in accord with your personal values and guiding principles, creates internal harmony.

As you continue to apply what you have learned in this program, your awareness of your TRUE SELF will continue to bolster your confidence and sense of security. Reflecting on this chapter should make you feel extremely good about what you have managed to accomplish in such a short period of time.

> With that in mind, I want you to do something very important. I want you to get into a state of...

Chapter 26 -

Celebration

Everyone likes to be rewarded for their efforts and accomplishments. Almost without exception, effort is motivated by the prospect of some kind of reward.

Rewards come in all shapes and sizes. Some have material value while others have emotional value. Most people go to work primarily for the material reward that comes in the form of a paycheck. Others, a happy minority, love what they do so much that the monetary reward is secondary to the feelings of accomplishment they experience.

When we do something nice for someone we love, our reward may be as simple as bringing a smile to their face. Making them feel good makes us happy, thus we are emotionally rewarded as well.

This action-reward feedback loop is an intrinsic part of human nature. It's closely related to the joy of giving, which is something we are going to cover in detail in the next section.

Here's what is important now. You have worked hard

to apply the information you've been learning and it's time to reward yourself. You need to complete the feedback loop.

Yes, elevating the quality of your life is rewarding. But what you really need now is to celebrate your accomplishments. Celebrating is one of the ways we give ourselves approval. You have just finished reflecting on your accomplishments. This is a perfect time to funnel massive amounts of approval into your neurological feedback loop.

Celebrating is an effective way to anchor your efforts in positive emotions. More approval brings increased motivation to continue taking action. Increased action creates more reason for giving yourself approval. It's a beautiful arrangement.

In his book "The 7 Habits of Highly Effective People" author Stephen R. Covey talks about a repeating upward spiral of personal growth. The sequence in his upward spiral is: learn → commit → do, which leads to the next level of learn → commit → do.

I agree with his analogy completely, but I would add one more element, approval. Without a built-in delivery system for receiving approval, motivation begins to fade. So my model for The Upward Expanding Spiral of Human Development would be:

learning → commitment → action → approval → and repeat

Commitment - Action - Approval - Learning - Commitment - Action

Learning - Commitment - Action - Approval - Learning

Approval - Learning - Commitment - Action - Approval

Action - Approval - Learning - Commitment - Action

Action - Approval - Learning - Commitment

Approval - Learning - Commitment

Learning - Commitment - Action

Personal development is a never-ending journey that pays giant dividends. Approval is the oil that keeps the whole process running smoothly.

So I'll say it one more time. Find a meaningful way to celebrate your accomplishments and let your newly transformed self know how much you approve.

"The more you praise and celebrate your life, the more there is in life to celebrate" -Oprah Winfrey

The reason the spiral is ever upward and ever expanding is because you were...

Chapter 27 -

Born to Succeed

One of the wonderful things about following a proven program for achieving our goals is that the whole process is repeatable. This is why very successful people can lose everything, and still come back to surpass their former level of success. They understand the process, they've done it before and they know they can do it again.

In fact, achieving success in any given field is generally much easier the second time around. There are several reasons for this.

First, you know the steps involved and having done it before, you know you can do it again. Second, success builds confidence and dispels doubt. Third, experience teaches you what to focus on, and what to avoid in order for you to speed the results.

This knowledge is also what allows successful people to compound their successes over and over again. After a while it becomes their natural tendency to succeed and that is exactly how it should be. Success in any endeavor feels good and natural on a core level. Underneath the low expectations that grow out of past failures and social programming, we all long to succeed in life. In truth, we are born to succeed and that's why it feels so satisfying when we do something right. It's our desired birthright.

How do we know that we are born with a desire to succeed?

Have you ever watched a baby learn to walk? Think about what's involved. Until a baby starts to walk, the only way he knows how to get from point A to point B, is to crawl. That's basically a four-legged mentality; it is a completely different set of motor skills and references than walking.

So what happens?

For starters, the parents help the baby to stand up while holding his arms. Then they rock him back and forth with some forward movement to try and simulate the walking experience. They are providing the child with a new perspective.

At first the baby doesn't understand what's going on. Then something clicks. All of a sudden the baby begins to relate to standing up, and now he <u>wants</u> to walk.

Walking becomes the baby's new goal and he is focused on it. Obviously, there is some preparation involved here, like learning how to stand up for more than two seconds, and learning how to take a step without falling down. Basically, it's a balance thing and it serves to help establish his new point of reference. We call it standing.

What are the parents doing this whole time? They become cheerleaders, encouraging the baby with words like "come on you can do it." They clap and get excited over the slightest bit of progress and the baby eats it up.

Then the decisive moment arrives; three consecutive steps, then five, then fifteen. It happens fast and our little friend is thrilled with his success.

Does it stop there?

No, because success brings more success. Within a very short time, that former crawler is running all over the place as fast as those little legs can move, because success feels great. You see we really are born to succeed.

Once we achieve a level of success, we should do three important things. The first is to feel a true sense of gratitude for all that we have been able to accomplish. The second is to celebrate. In doing so we should focus on enjoying the moment. Once you've reached your goal, give your mind and your loved ones a break.

Don't lose your balance and allow the desire to accomplish more become an obsession. Always strive to maintain a keen awareness of who you are right now, in this moment. Don't get caught up in compulsive accomplishment and forget who and what are really important to you.

After putting forth a highly focused effort, stop for a change of pace. Focus on family and friends. Spend time doing things that allow you to relax and regain your balance. If you don't do this you will drive yourself and everyone else crazy. Don't let yourself fall into the, "I haven't got time to take a break" trap. Make the time. You'll be happier and more productive if you do.

"Relaxation means releasing all concern
and tension and letting the natural order of life
flow through one's being." -Donald Curtis

Finally, once you are refreshed, ask yourself, what comes next? Set another goal, or group of goals, and start the process over again. Make success your habit.

Section Review

Internal conflict will always surface in the environment of success while internal harmony invites success.

Have you started paving the way to allow success into your life?

There are three core desires that influence everyone.

If you really want to enjoy genuine acknowledgment and feelings of deep approval, become very familiar with all three.

There are four important aspects included in the upward expanding spiral of human development.

Can you name some ways to give approval to yourself?

Achievement can be so energizing that it becomes easy to get out of balance.

What kind of activities can help us avoid this trap?

Section 7 – Fulfillment Connection

Life is Circular

About Section 7

Well, here we are at the seventh and final section, the fulfillment connection. So far, you have identified your core self and learned how to modify your beliefs. You've figured out exactly what success means to you personally and why.

You have also walked through the process of designing, planning, taking action and accomplishing your goals using a proven, systematic approach. And finally you learned how to identify with success and feel really good about allowing it into your life.

What's left? That's what you're about to discover as we explore ways to notch your personal growth and development up to the next level. It's time to embrace the number one way to magnify your sense of joy while simultaneously increasing the level of satisfaction you experience. Let's get started!

Chapters 28-30

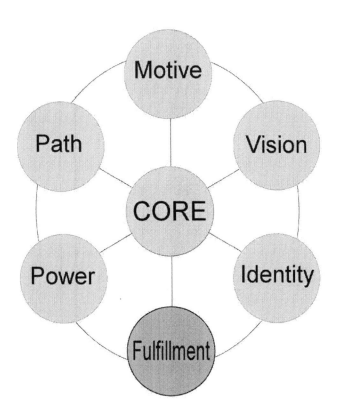

Chapter 28 -

Joy & Satisfaction

Mastering the advanced life skills in this program will completely change the way you experience your life. Having the personal resources to design success and then achieve your goals is really nothing short of transformational.

While appreciating that everyone would benefit from learning and applying these simple yet powerful techniques, the sad truth is, very few will. The reasons for this are the very same limiting beliefs that you have now learned to overcome.

This means that you now have something that others need. Do you know someone who lacks the emotional resources to meet life's challenges? I am sure you do.

So many people these days feel completely overwhelmed by the increasing demands in their daily lives. As a result, a considerable number are losing their ability to cope.

Emotionally, physically and financially people are being swallowed up because they have never been taught how to rise above their established response patterns and change their beliefs. They unknowingly live with internal conflict and disharmony.

How do you feel about the contrast in this area between your abundance and their lack? How should you feel? I cannot answer those questions for you. But I can show you how this imbalance creates an opportunity for you to take your personal growth to the next level. Here's a hint from a very reliable source:

> "There is more happiness in giving than there is in receiving" -Acts 20:35

Once you learn to fully apply the simple yet profound knowledge in this program, meeting your own challenges requires much less from you. Living in harmony with your personal values eliminates the internal conflict that keeps people feeling so off-balance and perplexed. What was once difficult for you has now become much easier and as a result, it has freed up a lot of energy and many of your emotional resources.

The next step in your personal development is to redirect a portion of your energy from self to others. You now have the ability to use your knowledge about human behavior to become a positive influence on those around you.

It's time to look for ways to contribute to family, friends and community. Freely giving of yourself to help others is truly a win-win situation. The more you can help others, the more you will help yourself. Or, as famous success coach *Jim Rohn* liked to put it:

> "Only by giving are you able to receive
> more than you already have"

Let's have another look at the Expanding Upward Spiral of Personal Development.

Notice how this spiral is smaller at the bottom and expands as it moves upward.

The bottom levels of personal development are mostly about you. If it were a circle it would continue to be about just you. But it is not a circle; it's a spiral that moves upward and outward.

Each trip around expands your world. In doing so it shifts an increasing percentage of your focus toward contributing to the lives of others. You can see how it looks on the next page.

- others – self – others – self – others – self – others -

Commitment - Action - Approval - Learning - Commitment - Action

Learning - Commitment - Action - Approval - Learning

Approval - Learning - Commitment - Action - Approval

Action - Approval - Learning - Commitment - Action

Action - Approval - Learning - Commitment

Approval - Learning - Commitment

Learning - Commitment - Action

self – self – self – self

At first glance it may seem that such a path would mean that your life would become less rewarding at each ascending level, as if contributing to others might somehow take away from your return on emotional investment. Actually, the exact opposite is true.

The rewards of selfish pursuits are extremely limited and empty. Whether we are aware of it or not, we all have a need to serve a greater cause than <u>self</u>. Deep down, it is part of our nature to want to help others, to make a positive difference in their lives.

Giving is the greatest source of joy and satisfaction known to humankind. This is a difficult concept to grasp when we are struggling to meet our own needs. Struggle and lack obscure our appreciation for giving. It's very difficult to give what we do not have.

Maybe you know that from personal experience. If so, you should be able to empathize with the plight of others. That is why the spiral is small at first. We need to give to ourselves before we will have something of value to contribute to others.

As we experience personal growth there is a natural shift that takes place. Not only will we have more to contribute, our desire to contribute also increases.

Once we begin to experiment with different ways of helping others, we will also discover a wide array of surprising benefits. It is absolutely true that helping others is a worthwhile pursuit all on its own, and that's exactly how we should view it. But in reality, most forms of giving also include receiving on some level.

Energy is constantly flowing to us and through us. It moves and changes as we receive it and then redistribute it. Giving actually increases the flow in both directions.

There is a special kind of satisfaction that comes only through contributing to others. In fact, I don't believe it is possible to experience a deeply satisfying and fulfilling life without a personal commitment to making valuable contributions.

A powerful internal transformation takes place once we embrace the role of a contributor. It initiates a deep level quantum shift in our values and beliefs. Our perception of what is important in life takes on a new dimension as our concept of reality begins to expand around the desire to help others.

A willingness to contribute should always be fueled by an unselfish desire to give without any thought of receiving something in return. True giving should come from the heart. Even so, those you help will often express gratitude.

Once your heart is touched by the grateful appreciation of another, you will be hooked on giving. The experience of receiving on that level expands your heart and changes your emotional identity.

In Chapter 24 we explored the three core emotions. Recall that a desire for security was the most compelling, followed closely by a desire for approval, and a desire for control. In the reference chart we laid out negative emotions that are rooted in insecurity and therefore should be avoided.

The positive side of this whole equation would be emotions which flow from and also encourage strong feelings of security, approval and control. Giving is directly related to, and supportive of these positive feelings. Notice how their relationship to one another is organized in the chart on the next page

Cultivating any of these feelings will help fulfill your most powerful desires, including the need to feel safe and secure. A true sense of security comes from within. Material assets are nice but the security they offer is fragile and shallow.

Giving is the most direct path to feeling a deep and meaningful sense of security. I encourage you to embrace and cultivate all of the emotions on the following chart. Their relationship to one another is synergistic, and collectively they represent a life of exceptional joy and satisfaction.

"Only those who have learned the power of sincere and selfless contribution experience life's deepest joy: true fulfillment."
-Anthony Robbins

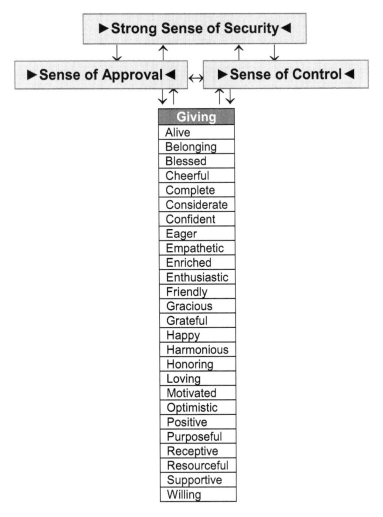

"There is no greater calling than to serve your fellow men. There is no greater contribution than to help the weak. There is no greater satisfaction than to have done it well." -Walter Reuther

Like everything else, giving is a skill. With practice we get better at it. Let's consider a few basics of...

Chapter 29 -

Contribution

As we continue, please keep in mind the concept of an expanding upward spiral as respects your personal growth and development. While dramatic changes can be accomplished very quickly, the overall process is one of consistent growth.

Using the techniques and strategies in this book have made it possible to initiate powerful shifts in your internal programming and focus. This process will often produce almost miraculous results. As you continue up the spiral however, change will not always occur so rapidly or be so obvious. Instead, it will be a fairly constant progressive upward transition.

Growth is by definition a continuing process involving subtle changes on the deepest levels. The visible evidence of these changes can take time to manifest. Of course, there will be periodic growth spurts, but continuous sustainable growth is the goal.

The transition from focusing on <u>self</u> to focusing on <u>others</u> should not be rushed or forced. As growth continues it will be the natural result of the personal development process. I have used the terms positive and negative reinforcement loop several times in this book and this is another example of a positive one.

A little progress provides the resources for a little giving, in turn the giving encourages more progress, and the progress leads to more giving. You cannot give what you do not have. Once you are filled to overflowing, giving and receiving are perpetual. Notice that a balance is always maintained between the two, as one increases so does the other. Balance is the key.

In our culture the term contribution is usually synonymous with the thought of monetary donations. Certainly there is nothing wrong with donating money to support a worthwhile cause. If you are in a position to do so, then by all means, make that one aspect of your personal program for giving. But do not limit yourself to this singular expression of contribution.

Experiencing the fullness of giving requires that we get personally involved. That means giving of ourselves, not just our material assets. Participation is preferred.

How can we do this?

Start where you live. If you have a family, start there! One of the reasons marriages fail is because one or both of the people involved has neglected the relationship. This is especially true where children are concerned. If your family falls apart, or your children self-destruct, one of the factors will likely be a lack of involvement. Make sure that you are giving your time and attention to your family in a meaningful way. They are worth it!

Outside of the family circle, friends are next in line. Friendship is a give-and-take arrangement. You have learned things that can help your friends to successfully deal with the challenges in their lives. How would it make you feel to help a friend over one of life's hurdles? Don't hold back from giving to those you care about.

> "Any person who contributes to prosperity
> must prosper in turn."-Earl Nightingale

In your neighborhood and community there are countless opportunities to contribute from your heart. Choose an area that appeals to you and get involved, not because you have to, but because you want to. Don't be afraid to open your heart to others!

People are losing their sense of community and withdrawing into their own isolated little worlds. Conditions in some areas may actually make this seem like the course of wisdom. However, minding your own business in some areas does not eliminate your ability to contribute in others. It's not about risking your life; it's about fellow feeling!

If you actively seek out ways to contribute, you will find them. When you do, ease into it with a small commitment of time and energy. See if it's a good fit. Contributing should be enjoyable and fulfilling, so make sure it is something you actually connect with.

You cannot fix every problem by giving of yourself. You are one person, so do what you can reasonably do, and feel good about it. If you take on more than you can handle, nobody will benefit. Your purpose in contributing is to become part of the solution and enjoy the experience, so be realistic.

Whatever avenue of giving you choose be sure to do it for the right reasons. When it comes to giving, motive is everything. If the desire to share in this way has not yet surfaced in your life, don't beat yourself up over it.

Continue to go through this program and build yourself up emotionally. When your own inner growth and development reaches a tipping point, contribution becomes the next logical step. Sooner or later you will get there; it is all part of the process. Change is part of growth. Anticipate it and then embrace it!   .

I can't say who made this quote, but they certainly had a good grasp of the big picture.

"Our inner strengths, experiences, and truths cannot be lost, destroyed, or taken away.

~

Every person has an inborn worth and can contribute to the human community.

~

We all can treat one another with dignity and respect, provide opportunities to grow toward our fullest lives and help one another discover and develop our unique gifts.

~

We each deserve this and we all can extend it to others." -Author Unknown

Are you wondering where we could possibly go from here? How about somewhere new but familiar…

Chapter 30 -

New Beginnings

At this point, please allow me to commend you and say congratulations. If you have made it this far, then you have successfully completed your first revolution on the Expanding Upward Spiral of Personal Development.

You have gone where few people dare to venture and that is something to feel extremely good about. Now that you have experienced the value of following a progressive program for personal growth, I hope you will make it a productive, lifelong pursuit.

With that in mind you might be wondering, what comes next?

You have not come to the end of this program, only to the first trip around the spiral. Instead of the finish, you have arrived back at the beginning.

We have all heard the expression "life's a circle." Allow me to make a slight alteration, "life is circular." Yes, you have come full circle but you have also ascended to the next level.

> "The secret to a rich life is to have more beginnings than endings." -David Weinbaum

How do you feel about your accomplishments so far? For my part, the opportunity to share with you has been truly meaningful. I have enjoyed it immensely.

Are you ready for round two? Don't forget to celebrate your achievements and give yourself approval first. Once you have done that, then it's time to go back to step one and start through the program again.

Even though the process is the same, each time you go through it is different, because it takes place on a different level of development. All of your internal references and beliefs will have changed since your last beginning. You are a different person now.

You may need to make some adjustments in your personal values and guiding principles. A change in perspective will alter your paradigms of pain and pleasure. This will also influence your choice of passions.

The truth is that everything from your beliefs about what is possible or important, to your goals and aspirations have probably undergone some degree of change. As we grow we change, and we will continue to change as we continue to grow. We can never experience anything the same way twice, because our awareness keeps evolving.

"There will come a time, when you believe everything is finished, that will be the beginning."
-Peter Nivio Zarlenga

That means that every time you begin this program, it is in fact a new beginning. After you have gone through this program a few times, stop and compare your current personal values, guiding principles and passions, with the ones you wrote down previously. You will likely be amazed at the changes that have occurred.

As we experience personal growth it is easy to forget how we used to feel. We lose track of what was important in the past, because we are focused on what is important now. Keeping a written record of your progress will create another legitimate reason to give yourself the approval that you truly deserve.

Having a proven, step-by-step process for setting and achieving goals is one of the surest ways to accomplish almost anything. Make certain to apply all the steps laid out for you in this program whenever you approach a new goal.

Chapters 14-17 systematically walk you through the planning phase of goal setting. Every time you even think about something you would like to accomplish, walk it through the process. This is the best place to add clarity and make adjustments. Always do this before you make a commitment and launch into action.

On the subject of action, where do you find yourself? Only by having the drive to make a commitment and act on it will you be able to benefit from what you have learned. Knowledge that is not followed by action is just so much data filed away and taking up valuable space.

To reap any real and lasting benefits from this program requires that you take action. You have in your possession a simple step-by-step guide for transforming your life. I have distilled it down to make it easy and fun for you. Most of the work is done.

The only thing I cannot do is take action for you. <u>That is entirely up to you!</u>

"Dreams pass into the reality of action.
From the actions stems the dream again;
and this interdependence produces the
highest form of living." -Anais Nin

If you have difficulty taking action, then you probably skipped over the exercises in step one. Perhaps you wanted to read through the rest of the program first to get your bearings. I completely understand because I tend to do the same thing.

But now you are at a crossroads. You can finish reading the program, set it aside and tell yourself that you will start working on it as soon as you have more time (wishful thinking). Or you can commit to getting started immediately (affirmative action).

I truly believe that you have what it takes to follow through. Thinking about the life you want to live is a good place to start. However, taking action is the only way to get there. Life is a journey we are all on together. Some choose to make it an endurance contest. I am so happy that you have chosen to make your life a wonderful adventure.

About the Author

By the time Jonathan Wells turned 22 he was living a lifestyle that probably seemed totally unrealistic to everyone he knew. He had completely abandoned his suburban roots to begin his own personal life quest.

Living deep in the forest of southern Oregon, Jonathan stripped his life down to the absolute bare minimum so he could start over from scratch. That's where his real life journey began.

More than three decades later Jonathan still loves being surrounded by nature. He considers himself to be an avid student of life, nothing more. He truly believes that living and learning should always go hand in hand and that we can all make a meaningful contribution by sharing what we learn along the way.

Over the years he has come to fully appreciate the incredible value that comes from connecting with your TRUE SELF. One of Jonathan's greatest passions in life is to help others make that connection. If you want to learn more about his life and work please visit Jonathan online at: AdvancedLifeSkills.com

More TRUE SELF

If you are looking to take your TRUE SELF journey to the next level, or if you want to share these valuable resources with a friend or loved one, you are cordially invite to visit TRUE SELF REVEALED online at:

TrueSelfRevealed.com

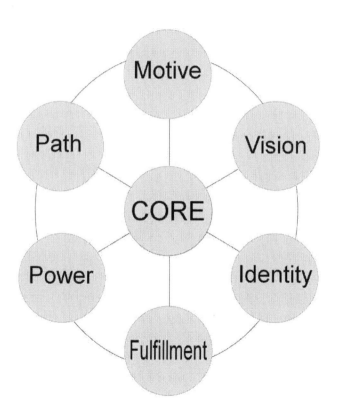

Made in the USA
Lexington, KY
14 January 2012